The Journeys of Faith, Hope, and Trust

Millicent Robinson

Outskirts Press, Inc.
Denver, Colorado

The opinions expressed in this manuscript are solely the opinions of the author and do not represent the opinions or thoughts of the publisher. The author represents and warrants that s/he either owns or has the legal right to publish all material in this book.

The Journeys of Faith, Hope, and Trust
All Rights Reserved.
Copyright © 2008 Millicent Robinson
V4.0

Cover Photo © 2008 JupiterImages Corporation. All rights reserved - used with permission.

This book may not be reproduced, transmitted, or stored in whole or in part by any means, including graphic, electronic, or mechanical without the express written consent of the publisher except in the case of brief quotations embodied in critical articles and reviews.

Outskirts Press, Inc.
http://www.outskirtspress.com

ISBN: 978-1-4327-2291-3

Outskirts Press and the "OP" logo are trademarks belonging to Outskirts Press, Inc.

PRINTED IN THE UNITED STATES OF AMERICA

Introduction

As we journey along life's pathway you may encounter with great difficulties, or some great task, whether through the wilderness, hardship of life, weakness of faith, through great sickness, or family conflicts, be not alarm "it only a test hold on." The hymnology encourages in shady green pastures so rich and so sweet God leads his dear children along where the water's cool flow bathes the weary one's feet Gods leads his dear children along. Some through the waters, some through the flood, some through the fire, but all through the blood; Some through great sorrow, but God gives a song; in the night season and all the day long. Bear in mind, that don't matter what the circumstances may be, God promise that he will never leave you alone. Be encourage that there is no mountain that's too high for God to bring down, there's no valley that's too low that God cannot pull you out of, there is just no sickness that is common around men that is too hard for God to heal, there is absolutely nothing too hard for God to do, he work on those things that seems impossible, and the things that seems difficult, or too hard for men to take care of he can fix it for you. See Matt.9:35, Mal.4:2, Ps.l03:3, Lu.8:47-48, David also made mentioned in Ps. 23:4 Yea, though I walk through the valley of the shadow of death, I will fear no evil for thou art with me, thy rod and thy staff they comfort me. Just never doubt God for nothing, trust him for your miracle, trust him for your healing, trust him for your deliverance, and trust him for every thing. When you trust God he will empower you and give you strength and authority. For those that put their trust in him shall never be ashamed. If you truly believe, your faith will make you whole. Brace yourself against every hardship, and the storms you may face in your life, for God's amazing power is a great legacy to those who love him and put their trust in him.

From the Author

The contents of this book is a true testimony of the Author, as you take the time out to read this book may you find it to be of great inspiration to your soul, food for thought, a multi-vitamin for the inner being, may it fill your heart with joy as the fresh dew that comes down from on high, as you will see God from a diligent aspect. Knowing that God still works miracles, he who still do wonders among his children, a God that will fight each of your battle until they are won, knowing that the weapon of our warfare are not carnal but mighty through God to the pulling down of strong holds; Casting down imaginations, and every high thing exalteth itself against the knowledge of God and bring into captivity every thought to the obedience of Christ 2Cor.9:4-5. He is a God that cares when no one else seems to care, because he can be touch with the feeling of our infirmities, a God that have all the answers for every problems and situations. Keeping this in mind when you are feeling down and out, just remember that God is always up and around, Ps. 125: 1-4 They that trust in the Lord shall be as mount Zion which cannot be removed, but abideth for ever. As the mountains are around about Jerusalem, so the Lord is round about his people from henceforth even for ever. For the rod of the wicked shall not rest upon the lot of the righteous ; lest the righteous put forth their hands unto iniquity, remember that God will surly do good to those that be good and to them that are upright in hearts.

Acknowledgements

This book is highly dedicated to my dear loving mother Seleta Plummer who has been the charm of my life, a great mentor, who have brought me up and nature me in the fare and knowledge and wisdom of God, one that I can never repay for what she have done for me no matter how hard I may try. One that know how to abase, and abound, a generous and profound woman of God, one that knows how to give God thanks for much, or plenty, or even when there is none at all, through the rain, and the sunshine, through the boisterous storm, even through hurricane Dean which recently left her homeless, but not hopeless, she's still that mom with a gentle smile giving the almighty thanks for sustaining her life.

To my brother Altiman who is surviving terminal cancer, My Pastor Bishop & overseer E. R. Thomas, First Lady, M Thomas, Maxine Samuels, Dian Gayle, Andrae Brackett, Ann-marie Peart, Rest Tabernacle at large.

To my loving husband Joshua Robinson, and my two

daughters Elysia, & Lachane, & my only son Shaquille Jamall thanks for putting up with me during my time of illness thanks, I couldn't have done it with out you.

To all my Siblings: Mavis, Alice, Winniefred, Sylvia, Hilda, Joyce, and Vincent. Thanks, thanks, thanks, may the good Lord bless you all real good.

Prove Your God

- A God who's love is with out boundaries
- Whose love is binding, and his mercies unfading
- He who listen while you pray and turn your darkness in to day
- A great battle –axe
- A shelter from the storm.
- A God that knows it all

Profile

Missionary Millicent Robinson is a member of Rest tabernacle Church of Jesus Christ Apostolic of Toronto Canada. Under the Pastor ship of Bishop E.R. Thomas.

A true believer of Jesus Christ, both "**grounded and settled** "in the teaching, walking, and living in the realms of God's eternal word, with the assurance of His future glory and eternal life.

Called to be an intercessor, as I intercede in fasting and prayer working with others for their deliverance.

It is my most earnest endeavor to share this **Gospel** to every nation.

Hope Scripture Reading:

St John 3; 3
I peter 3:15
II timothy 2:16
Titus 1:2
Titus 2:13
Colossian 1:5
Colossians 1:37
I timothy 5:8
Ephesians 2:12
I Corinthians 15:19
II Corinthians 1:7
II Corinthians 3:12
Romans 8; 24

Trust Scripture Reading:

Job 13:15
Psalms 25:22
Psalms 118:8
Proverbs 28:26
Matthew 27:43
Luke 18:9
I Timothy 4:10

Faith Scripture Reading:

Acts 13:9
Romans 5:1
II Corinthians 5:7
James 5:15
Matthew 6:30
Matthew 21:21
Hab 2:4
Acts 6:5
Hebrews 11:1
Hebrews 4:2

This is Part One

The New Man

Christian are brand new people on the inside. The Holy Spirit gives us new life and we are not the same anymore. We are not reformed, rehabilitated or reeducated, we are recreated. 2 Cor.5:17 says "Therefore, if any man be in Christ, he is a new creature: old things are passed away; behold, all things are become new." Therefore, as a new creation, we are living in vital union with Christ. We are not merely turning a new leaf; we are beginning a new life under a new master. Meaning, that our old way of life (before we believed in Christ) is completely in the past; we put it behind us like clothes to be thrown away. This is both a once–and–for–all decision (when we decide to accept Christ's gift of salvation) and also a daily conscious commitment. We are not to be driven by desire and impulse but we must put on the new role, head in the right direction and have the new way of thinking that the Holy Spirit gives. God brings us to himself by blotting out our sins and making us righteous; we are no longer God's enemies, strangers to him or foreigners to him when we trust in him. Because we have been reconciled to God, we have the privilege of encouraging others to do the same; we are those who have the ministry of reconciliation.

Christian's Lifestyle

Christians are free to be all they want to be for God, but not free from God. Humanity was created in the image and likeness of God. Yes he created both male and female. (Gen 2:6-27).

God created sex to be a beautiful and essential ingredient to marriage but sex outside of marriage is sin. Sex outside of a marriage relationship always hurts someone, especially God and the church. It hurts God because it shows that we prefer to follow our own ways and desires instead of the leading of the Holy Spirit. It hurts the church or others because it violates the commitment and the ordinance pertaining to true holiness. Col. 3:5 tells us that we should mortify our members, which is upon the earth.

Meaning, that we should consider ourselves dead and unresponsive to sexual immorality, uncleanness, inordinate passion and evil desires as these are some of sins diseases and they will destroy us as Cancer to the physical body.

Should you be practicing such, or even allowing the thought of it, put those thoughts away before we are destroyed by them.

As James 1:15 reminds us that when lust hath conceived it bringeth forth sin, and sin, when it is finished, bringeth forth death. It's a must that we make a conscious daily decision to remove any or everything that supports or feeds these desires.

We should rely on the Holy Spirit as well as the words of God. Ps: 119:11 said, "Thy word have I hid in mine heart, that I might not sin against thee." Some may say they have the right to do whatever they want with there own bodies but we are not our own but God's property. Although tempted and tried by our adversary, the devil, that old deceiver, the wicked one, we must remember that Jesus Christ himself was tempted on several occasions but yet without sin. (Matt 4:1, Mk 1:13).

The apostle Paul also encouraged the Corinthians in 1 Cor. 10:13 "There hath no temptation taken you but such as is common to man: but God is faithful, who will not suffer us to be tempted above that ye are able; but will with the temptation also make a way to escape, that ye may be able to bear it." So when we are tempted to sin, we must remember that one day we shall stand before God who will judge us accordingly. Wrong desires and temptations happen to every one of us, so don't feel you've been singled out. Any temptation can be resisted because God will help us to resist it, by recognizing the people, things or situations that give us trouble. Having acknowledged the problems, walk away from it and choose to do only what is right. We then must begin to pray for God's help, seek new friends who love God and who can offer help when you are tempted. Just remember when you've walked away from any temptation you are on your way to victory.

Restoring Relationship With God

Restore means to return to your former righteous state, or to reinstate to your former position. It may not be easy at first because trust has been broken. When a trust is broken situations change but with true repentance, submission, prayer and fasting God will forgive. Generally, man looks at the outward appearance but only God can see the heart. With a broken and a contrite heart God will not despise. Although God has forgiven you, the situation still remains in the eyes of men because it is not the ninety – nine good deeds that you have done in the sight of men that are cherished but rather the one mistake that you have done is kept in memory. But remember God is the only one that has the last word, so do as Paul said look for the old path and when you find it walk therein. At times it might seem that God is silent. By his silence, he is not condoning sin nor is he indifferent to it; instead he is withholding deserved punishment, giving time for people to repent. 2 Pt. 3:9 remind us, that God takes no pleasure in the death of the wicked and wants them to turn from evil.

Ps. 51 also reminded us of King David; when his silence was discovered by God, he was truly sorry for his adultery with Bathsheba and for murdering her husband to cover it up. He knew that his actions had hurt many people but because David repented of those sins, God mercifully forgave him. No sin is too great to forgive. Do you feel that you could never come close to God because you have done something terrible? God can and will forgive you of any sin. While God forgives us, he does not always erase the natural consequences of our sin. David's life and family were never the same as a result of what he had done (2 Sam.12:1-23).

Do you ever feel stagnant in your faith, as though you are just going through the motions? Has sin ever driven a wedge between you and God, making him feel distant? I do believe that David felt this way. He had sinned with Bathsheba and had just been confronted by Nathan the prophet. In his prayer he cried to the Lord, asked that the joy of his salvation be restored unto him. God wants us to be close to him and to experience a full and complete life. But, when we have sins that remain un-confessed it makes such intimacy impossible. Confess all your sins to God; you may still have to face some earthly consequences, as David did; however, it will be worth it in the end. When God forgives our sins and restores us to a relationship with him, we want to reach out to others who need this forgiveness and reconciliation.

Committed To Truth

*W*ords are powerful and how we use them reflects on our relationship with God; as a Christian we should know how to control our speech. Speaking truth means refusing to slander, keeping promises, watching out for what we say. Don't exaggerate statistic, pass on rumors, gossip or create stories to buildup your own image, but rather commit your self to be truthful and your soul shall live thereby. St. Jn. 8:32 - "Ye shall know the truth and the truth shall make you free." Someone may say a little white lie is a good thing, but there is no such thing as a white lie. We may try to lie to ourselves to suit a situation, but instead it turns around and sinks us deeper into the problem. As I can remember some time ago, I had to attend an emergency conflict meeting. Whatever was said in the meeting was to remain confidential but someone (who just could not keep their tongue in control) went and violated the privacy; then the rumors and gossip started. I was the one who was accused of violating the privacy. I was quite upset, I mean very upset. It didn't matter how I tried, they wouldn't accepted the truth. In the midst of it all, someone dropped a word in my spirit "Blessed are ye when men revile you and persecute you and shall say all manner of evil against you falsely, for my sake (Matt. 5:11)."

Here is another experience. I was coming from school, me and two of my friends were waiting for the school bus, and as we stood there, they were gossiping over a situation they had with one of my cousin. I was standing there with my mouth shut. Never a part-taker in their conversation, one of them said to me 'you aren't saying anything and it doesn't mean you aren't with us'; I still did not say a word. A few days later they came accusing me, stating everything that was said in my presence all went back to my cousin's ears and it had to be me who told her. I kept my cool because I knew I did not mention a word to her. It didn't matter what I said to those two girls, they strongly believed that I was the one who brought back words to my cousin. Sometimes it doesn't matter what we do or say, some people will not believe or accept the truth. Just remember the truth will always stand out; the truth will always make your heart and mind free. Maybe at work dealing with co-workers, at school with your friends with similar situations or experiencing even worst, just remember God is always there looking out for you. God's words are binding; it's powerful and it can control our minds.

You Are Labeled

When we become a Christian, we become labeled for Christ. The world looks at us differently; they watch our every move. We are a speckle bird. We are judged by our walking, actions, speech, places we go, you name it…

People are looking for mentors, for others to guide them to Christ. As Christians, let's take extra precautions so that we will not block their entrance to Christ.

Being labeled as a "Christian" is our identification from earth to heaven, it is a description of our life and we should walk with it everywhere we go. Someone noted, I must have the savior with me for I dare not walk alone, I must feel his presence near me and his arms around me thrown. Act 11:26 tells us that the church was first called Christians in Antioch because they worshipped Christ. Calling them Christians did not mean they approved of their love for

Christ but they were making fun of them, despising or ridiculing them. So don't feel a bit discouraged when the world despises you, laughs at you and calls you names. Just feel blessed, feel special because you are dressed in the likeness of God.

John 2:13 reminds us that we should not marvel if the world hates us. Sometimes our mind takes us on a wild chase; we forget the manner of person we ought to be. We may feel pressured a times to apologize when we do wrong and, even if we are asked to make an apology, we think within ourselves that it is not necessary. When we hurt someone's feelings we think it should be ok; not considering ourselves. We become angry when we are corrected because we feel inferior to be corrected. We become rebellious in our minds when we hear the truth because speaking the truth doesn't mean much to us. Does any of these sounds familiar? If yes, then start checking your label and make some amendments, if you consider yourself to be on the right track. It is of vital importance for us to do continuous self examinations daily, or as often as possible, because the heart of a human can become exceedingly corrupt. Jer.17:9 declares unto us that the heart is deceitful above all things, and desperately wicked; who can know it? God made it very clear why we sin; it's a matter of the heart. Our hearts have being inclined towards sin from the time we were born. It is very easy to fall into the routine of forgetting God, but we can still choose whether or not to continue in sin. We can yield to a specific temptation, or we can ask God to help us resist temptation when we are face with them. Let us also be reminded that there is a reward for whatever choice we make in our lives. "For the wages of sin is death, but the gift of God is eternal life" (Rom. 6:23).

Let us ask God to search us, try our hearts, change all the wicked ways in us, cleanse our hearts from every sin and make us free. We do not want to represent the wrong product nor be a good label with contaminated product. Let's be what we ought to be as we do not want to be misrepresentatives of heaven because heaven is a holy place, filled with God's glory and grace a place where there is no room for sin.

In today's society lots of people are very concerned about their health, they are so careful of what they consume, for sure. When they get to the grocery stores, they take extra precaution with the ingredients in every item before putting it in the shopping cart. We want to be sure the label is correct, the product is healthy and we are getting a reasonable price.

I was watching the news sometime ago and, to my knowledge, there was a home owner that had a very bad experience, with bad weed taking over his lawn. His intention was to get rid of the bad weeds, so he went to the store pick up a container of weed-killer I can imagine how happy he was just thinking of how beautiful his lawn would be after he cured it of the bad weeds. It so happened, that after he sprayed the lawn a few days later he found the complete lawn was destroyed. After checking the label on the container he realized that he had bought the wrong product. By this time he was so embraced, he did not want to appear before the Media camera. Unfortunately, now he will have to remove the entire lawn and replace it all.

Thinking back about the situation it makes me wonder how costly a misread label can be.

If he had takes the time to read the label on the container it would have cost him less money to care for his lawn. Failing to do so, cost him a lot more in unexpected spending and time that could have been avoided; not to mention the embracement.

As Christians, let us be very careful of the life we portray and the services we give; for the lives we live will surly speak for us. When we mislabel ourselves we give people the wrong impression about Christians, and will block their entrance to salvation. There is always a cost to re-instate ourselves to the right position.

Blessed is the man that walketh not in the council of the ungodly nor standeth in the way of sinners nor sitteth in the seat of the scornful. (Ps. 1:1) We have to be very careful as Christians because we are surrounded by sin every moment of the day, therefore we should let our minds be centered on Christ. As reminded in Ps. 51:5, we are born in sin and shapen in iniquity and in sin did our mothers conceive us.

So you can see we didn't have to be indulging wrongs to go to hell, because we were born in it (sin). When we become mature to know the

difference between wrong and right, we should make the choice to walk with Christ the Lord, make the choice to be loyal and true to God. Endeavor to keep your heart and mind pure by meditating, singing onto the Lord in songs and scripture, hymn, making melody in your hearts.

1 John 3:12, reminds us of Cain and Abel, Cain had a label which identified him spiritually as a child of the devil. His act of murder was the epitome of hatred, so jealousy and anger drove him to murder. His brother, Abel, also had a label which identified him as a child of God. It is very important you know your identity, you cannot be a subsidiary. When you appear before the mirror, you see not two people but yourself. Seems then we cannot hide from the almighty God. Let us measure up ourselves with the word, the closer we get to God the more our undone state appears. However, the bible reads that our best state before him is as filthy rags. Let us continue to seek God's face knowing that he is righteous and holy. Break up our folly ground and abide with the Lord until he comes and rains righteousness upon us. My encouragement to us-ward, touching the daily challenge for every person seeking to live for God is this:

do not grow weary of righteousness. Herein lays the secret of being ready for Christ's return.

If the hope of his arrival stirs up a whole hearted commitment to do good for his sake, we will be ready for him as we must be busy waiting.

Love And Affection For Others

Love is a strong affection, or warm attachment. Love is also loyal and unselfish meaning you don't always wait, expecting love to come to you, but rather you will have to seek love, or reach-out towards love. There is always a complaint; nobody loves me, or no one cares about me, but have you reached out to that someone, or those some ones, and tried to entertain the entrance of love? Love has no width or breadth but in every category of love, where we are categorized, we should be able to fill in. We should not allow our love to be restricted to any one, nation, or to any spiritual elite, even to those that hate you and despitefully use you. So then, love should be without boundary. Referring to God's love, it is not static or self centered but it reaches out and draws others in. Here God sets the pattern of true love; the basis for all love relationship. When you love some one dearly, you're willing to give freely to the point of self-sacrifice, or willing to go the extra mile; some times even if it costs life.

We know that God paid dearly, with the life of his son, the highest he could pay. 'O what a love'? As Jn. 3:16 referred, for God so love the world that he gave his only begotten son, that whosoever believeth in him should not perish but have everlasting life. Therefore, Jesus Christ accepted our punishment by paying the price for our sin. So he offered to us the new life that he had bought for us. I am so glad for this new life, aren't you? When we share the good news to others, we must portray the love of Jesus Christ. We should be willing to give up our own comfort and security so that others might join us in receiving eternal life. Some people may feel repulsed by the idea of eternal life, because their lives are miserable, but eternal life is not an extension of a person's misery or moral life; eternal life is God's life, embodied in Christ, which he gave to all who believeth in him. Whosoever abideth in him shall inherit eternal life. Sometimes we may experience obstacles in our way, but let us see them as stepping stones to glory; where we will be free from stress, sickness, cancer (that is the #1 killer), pain, evil, bills, sin or death. For we step into eternal life with Jesus Christ. As quoted in 1 Cor. 15, if in this life only we have hope in Christ, we are like men most miserable. This present life is just the introduction to eternal life which can be only found in Jesus Christ the Lord alone, who died that we might have life more abundantly. If you have not yet received Christ Jesus, just open up your heart towards him and receive this new life; begin to evaluate all that can happen from an eternal perspective.

You Are Special

Every child should be loved and cared for in a very special way. Every child should feel that they are wanted among their families; although, that doesn't seems to happen all the time.

Some children are less fortunate in this case, some are abused and neglected by parents, some run away from home, while others have been abandoned.

I truly would like all children to know that they are very special. Don't matter what culture or nationality you are. God made you special. Don't feel that through neglectfulness you should feel unwanted, uncomfortable or for any other reason should you feel discouraged; you are very special in the sight of God.

Parents are usually the best judge of their children's character, they can summarize their personalities. Some children usually have good intentions but seem unable to express him or her self accordingly, or unable to stand against a crowd; so then their instability may seem somewhat hard. They might have some private and/or public skills which are of great values, but there is a contrast, they contradicted each other.

There are folks with great potential, or ability, but unable to portray it. They may be underprivileged because of their culture, or race. However, it should be every parent's dream to see their children exceed the highest goal or to reach the unreachable stars. Some parents established their children's goal setting, as an investment, as they nurture and grow. (See Pro. 22:6) Train up a child in the way he should go and when he is old he will not depart from it.

To most parents, their children are their number one priority. They will go to any extreme to give their children the proper education. Trust me, they will spend the last dime, borrow loans, credit cards or even mortgage their homes. There are many parents who were under privileged and unable to get to a good education, because their parents were very poor and unable to assist them financially. As a result, some had dropped out of school, to find employment in order to help their parents financially and also to further their education.

Today's parents have other goals set; they wanted to make sure their children achieve things in life that were not privileged to receive.

Expect To Be Targeted At Because You Are Special

I thought of Joseph because he was the second youngest child of twelve brothers and he was also his father's favorite child. (See Gen. 32:33). He must have felt overconfident and some times, probably would've bragged to himself about his dreams and his special coat of many colors; as other children would do. I know what it is be categorize in this situation, being the youngest child in my family. I had some great privileges being called the baby in the family, daddy's, pet, my parents favorite (still am) and always getting away with everything. When I did something wrong, I would cry or run and hide underneath the bed. I know I wouldn't be spanked; however, I still wanted to be pampered.

This was just in my world; Joseph's world was so much different. His father's love and favoritism almost cost him his life. Favoritism in families may not be avoidable but the divisive effects should be minimized. Parents may not be able to change their feelings towards a favorite child, but they can change actions, towards the other.

As a youngster, Joseph was overconfident. His natural self assurance increased by being Jacob's favorite son and by knowing of God's design on his life. This was unbearable to his ten brothers, who eventually conspired against him. But his self-assurance molded by pain and combined with a personal knowledge of God, allowed him to survive and prospers where most would have failed.

He added a lot of quite wisdom to his confidence and won the heart of everyone he met. (Gen. 37:6-11). When you are targeted, your enemies will try all means and ways to harm you, but God has your back covered under his wings of protection.

Maybe you can identify with one or more of that hardship Joseph experienced; he was betrayed and deserted by his family, exposed to sexual temptation and punishment for doing the right thing, he endured a long imprisonment and was forgotten by those he helped. But in each case, Joseph's positive response transformed each setback into a step forward. I don't believe he had spent much time asking "Why"; it is likely that his approach was, "what shall I do now?"

Those who met Joseph were aware that wherever he goes or whatever he does God was with him. Should you be prefacing a setback, the beginning of a Joseph like situation, it is for you to acknowledge that God is with you and tests only come to make you stronger. Just remember you're targeted every day but you can be an over-comer.

God has anointed you and blessed you. Never mind the arrows that are pointed at you, they shall not harm you; have confidence in your defender. Joseph was young but had a positive desire for God. (Gen. 39:7-1) When he was exposed to sexual advances he said 'how can I do this great wickedness and sin against my God'. Joseph's brothers were very angry of the fact that there was a possibility that their younger brother would rule over them, according to the interpretation of his dreams. Maybe they were jealous of him or covetous but there cometh also envy and strife which leads to murder. May be they were asking the questions "why not me? Why him?" These are all sinful deeds and action, bad spirits that dwells among us. If they enter into us it germinates in our hearts, our minds, and thoughts; ready to destroy us if we yield to them. Then, cometh sin because out of the abundance of the hearts cometh both good thoughts and evil thoughts.

Let us be aware lest we get caught up in the same situation.

God is in control and God uses who he pleases. It doesn't matter who you really are or what position you occupy. God needs his job to be accomplished. You must be qualified for such accomplishment. You must be clean and ready, washed and holy, pure and sanctified; a prepared vessel for the master's use, having your minds cleansed from an evil conscience. Heb. 10:22 said "Let us draw near with a true heart in full assurance of faith, having our hearts sprinkled from an evil conscience, and our bodies washed with pure water." So be prepared for the master's job. So when you get into God's sanctuary get focused, put away note pads, avoid moving from your seat (unless you're being distracted), rest a while from socializing, turn off the cell phones (they too can be distractive). Tell the devil 'I am not here for a show but I am here to worship God. I am here to send some praises to the most high God.' You are anointed and being empowered by God, you could be the

Pastor, any Rostrum Associate, the Choir or the Praise and Worship Group, a Worshiper in the congregation or someone in the Amen Corner; it could be you or it could be me, just be prepared and ready to serve. When the devil casts sleep upon you, tiredness, or slumber-ness upon you, stand up and start worshiping. The devil only wants to steal your strength, when you're sleeping you won't get to hear the word of God and that's where you get your spiritual strength. The multi vitamin for the soul.

Pr. 6:10-11 states "Yet a little sleep, a little slumber, a little folding of the hands to sleep: So shall thy poverty come as one that traveleth, and thy want as an armed man."

Let no devil steal your praise, your testimonies, your joy, your strength, your worship, your peace or your mind.

Be radical for God. David made mention in Ps 100:4 "Enter into his gates with thanksgiving, and into his courts with praise: be thankful unto him, and bless his name."

God's calling is already pronounced upon your life, so see each target as just another stepping stone. The devil is aware of your potential; he is very devious, cunning and tricky. So, arm yourself and be on the alert for that opposer; don't be naive. If sinners entice you consent thou not. You may be young but maintain your integrity. You might be told many times how beautiful you are or how handsome you look, but you already know who you are, be your own mirror. Be committed for God he has a plan working out for you. In that plan there is a package; that package is fully loaded with that sanctified husband, the virtuous wife, the job you've being waiting for, that car you needed so badly, the financial needs, that nice home; only trust God and wait in faith. So think about that beautiful smile before you give it, sometimes all the devil wants is just that smile, which could be a target for you. Think about the promotion before you accept the offer, although you need that extra cash sometimes there is a target behind the promotion. Think about the dinner dates, the lunch dates, the car rides, the emails and phone calls the job offers. Just be careful before you give in. There was a time when I was targeted by a so called "doctor", by responding to an ad in the Toronto star to fill the position as a doctor's secretary. I was so amazed and delighted when I was told that I could come in for an interview the same day, he made mention that he operates a Clinic, but all interviews were done at his house. Maybe I was naive here, or impolite, for not asking why at the house; however, I went to the interview which was done in a professional manner. When it was time for salary arrangements, he stated he has several secretaries at the clinic but he would like me to be his main secretary answering all his personal calls, making his reservations and to be sure that his coffee is on his desk. He let me know that my salary would be different from the rest and that it should be private and confidential. Last but not least, he said "I travel to Miami every two weeks and I would like to have you as my traveling partner". I responded, "Thanks very much for your offer, it sound very challenging but I don't believe am the right person for this job. My reason being is that I am the general recording secretary at my church plus I am engaged in several other activities at my church. He responded 'Oh, I'm so sorry; you seemed to be the right person for the job.' He got up from his chair and so did I (because at the close of an interview both party would stand and give a hand shake). Instead, he stretched his hand towards my arm. Rude! How dare he put his hand on me! I took my handbag and walked out the house hastily. Even up to this present day it is questionable if this man really had a job to offer or if it was just his corrupt practice. The next day was fasting service at church and I was the moderator so I drew their attention to the ad so that they wouldn't respond to it.

What ever this man had in mind was not accomplished because I shunned the very appearance of evil.

Youth Is The Time To Seek God

We often here people say "It doesn't matter" but many of your choices will be irrevocable; they will stay with you for a life time.

What you do when you're young does matter. Enjoy life now, but don't do anything physically, morally or spiritually that will prevent you from enjoying life when you are old. Ecc. 12 gives us a reminder to "Remember now thy Creator in the days of your youth, while the evil days come not, nor the years draw nigh, when thou shall say, I have no pleasure in them." A life without God can produce a bitter, lonely and hopeless old age. A life centered on God is fulfilling. It will bring you through the difficult days, when disabilities, sickness and handicaps cause barriers to enjoying life. Being young is very exciting, lots of fun, lots of privileges and lots of opportunities; but the excitement of youth can become a barrier to closeness with God if it makes young people focus on passing pleasures instead of eternal resources to be. Make your strength available to God, when it is still yours. During your youthful years, don't waste it on evil or meaningless activities that can become bad habits and makes you callous. Seek God now; death is no respecter of person, or age. We realize how easily death comes to us, how swiftly and unexpectedly we can return to the dust from which we came. Therefore, we should recognize life as a precious resource to be used wisely and not squandered frivolously. When you get the chance, please use up your resources wisely. Be an evangelist, a missionary, be soul focused; you don't have to be ordained to be soul focused. Take a little time out for God at break time, lunch time, at school or at work. Invite someone to church on Sundays, at Convocation or at conferences. Share even a verse of scripture with them; to those that will hear or listen to you. Target yourself to even one soul per month you will be doing some good on your part and you will be adding to your account. You could also open a new account named "Soul winners for Christ" (SWC)

Many youngsters are dying, dropping as dead flies or as birds and hunted like wild animals in the forest; gone without a hope of eternal life. My God "What a waste"? Some are faced with deadly diseases like cancer, AIDS, you name it. We are terrified when these conditions or symptom are being diagnosed.

I remember as a youth growing up I would evangelize to my peers at school and I would invite them to church. Some attended, heard the word and gave their lives to the Lord but other refused to accept the call into eternal life while some never showed up. However, I have made sure I was doing my part in sharing the good news of salvation and eternal life. This we should know that when we are stripped of God's spirit, our bodies return to dust, stripped of God's purpose, our work is in-vain, stripped of Gods love, our services are futile. Put God first in whatever you do because without him we have nothing. There are endless opinions about life and philosophies about how we should live that we could read and study forever; however, it is not wrong to study these opinions, but we should spent the majority of our time feeding on the truth of God's word of which you let wisdom lead you into action. A wise bible student will understand and do whatever they have being taught. Because our time on earth is so short, we should use it wisely to learn important truths.

There is an antidote for those who are seeking for God's purpose and direction in their life: to fear God and keep his commandments. Those who think that life is unfair should remember that God will review every person's life and will determine how he or she responds to him. He promises to bring every work into judgment. Have you committed your life to God, both present and future? No matter what the mysteries and apparent contradictions of life are, we must work towards the single purpose of knowing God. Let us acknowledge the evil, foolishness and injustice in life, yet, we should maintain a positive attitude and strong faith in God knowing that God will judge the quality of every person life.

Seek ye the Lord while he may be found, call ye upon him while he is near: Let the wicked forsake his way, and the unrighteous man his thoughts: and let him return unto the Lord, and he will have mercy upon him; and to our God, for he will abundantly pardon. (Isa. 55:6-7)

All believers need in-depth teaching so that they may know how to nurture and maintain the unity of the church and to keep themselves un-spotted from the unrighteous things of this world. God wants us to keep all important information in our minds so that when we are too busy to read our bible, we can go to our file and click on our memory box. What do you think will come back to memory? A dynamic message you heard some Sunday's ago that was such a blessing to your soul, something uplifting you could not resist meditating on it, or even a testimony you heard that strengthened you, maybe a song that the Praise and Worship group sang which inspired your soul (you also click on that too). Then send a message back to your memory box in thanksgiving. Somebody might think you're crazy but of course you're not; just contents under pressure needing to explode. Have you ever been going on the highway and suddenly God's glory comes down on you? My God, you feel like stopping the vehicle and shouting praises to God; this will happened when you are in His presence. Ps. 16:11 declares that "in thy presence is fullness of joy; at thy right hand there are pleasures forevermore." To him be all praise; given to him who has blessed us with every spiritual blessing in heavenly places. It is so good to know that we have all the benefits of knowing God, being chosen for salvation, being adopted as his children, forgiveness in his sight, the gift of the spirit, power to do God's will and the hope of living forever with Christ. "Bless God" what a package! We are fully loaded. I am truly bless, what about you?

Because we have an intimate relationship with God, we can enjoy these blessing now. Just think how blessed you are. The heavenly places means that these blessings are eternal not temporal. The bible tells us that we were chosen in him before the foundation of the world, and that we should be holy and without blemish before him in love. So seeing that Christ has chosen us in him, what a mystery? To emphasize that salvation depends totally on God, we are not save because we deserve it but because God is gracious towards us.

He freely gives salvation, we did not negotiate with God nor did we influence his decision to save us; he saved us according to his plans. Therefore, let us humble ourselves and do not give room to pride for pride cometh before destruction. Let us rather give credit to our Lord Jesus Christ, who has given to us this wonderful salvation. Just imagine, in the timeless mind of God, long before we were existed, it sometimes seems hard to understand how God could accept us, pay the penalty for our sin and forgive us. We have been reconciled, brought near to him. We are a new society, a new family, being united with Christ. So, it is for us to treat each other as family members, seeing that God has chosen us and adopted us as his own children and made us heirs along with Jesus. (Ro. 8:17) Did you know that adopted children have the same rights and privileges as biological children? So are you. You are privileged to have a strong bond in this relationship. If you are not yet in his family, get adopted. There is room at the cross for you.

Blessings On Your Obedience

You will always be rewarded greatly when you yield yourself to God's word in obedience. Deut. 28:1 said, if you diligently obey the voice of the Lord your God to observe carefully all his commandments which I command you this day, that the lord your God will set you high above all nations of the earth.

We should take a moment and consider the work force environment today; management are very careful of whom they give promotions.

They look for people with high potential, one that works under pressure, a multi-tasker, a leader and one who demonstrates willingness, productivity, growth, punctuality, honesty and proper attiring. These are some of the qualities and skills employers look forward to seeing in an employee. When you are furnished with those qualities, you may be up for promotions. Sometimes, because of favoritism, management doesn't always work this way. But when the wrong man is in the wrong position, then productivity goes down, so do sales, then total loss followed by bankruptcy.

But when the right person is the right position then business will excel, there will be excess sales, profits, bonuses and overtime. In the learning institutions, you may have teacher and professors who may put out every effort to bring out the top quality or best in their students. Successful scholars in their own prospective or most dignified manner, however, it is the student's own initiative to pursue towards their own intensive goal. In the church realm, God sets out his commandments for men of all races, great and small, rich and poor, Jew and Gentiles, bond and free.

In addition, there are great rewards to be accomplished. This accomplishment is signified as a bonus or blessing on your obedience. To be blessed is a bestowal of God's divine favor and benefits. Gen.1:22, 9:1-7 which also include recognition of God's goodness, in a thankful and adoring manner, and what Noah received abides in you, which will give you that motivation to be submissive, respective or make a difference to men of high degree as well as men of low degree. Gen 22:15-18 reminds us how Abraham received abundant blessings because he did not hold back but obeyed God. God gave Abraham's descendants the ability to conquer their enemies. God said to him in blessing I will bless thee, and in multiplying I will multiply thy seed as the stars of the heaven, and as the sand which is upon the sea shore. And in thy seed shall all the nations of the earth be blessed, because thou hast obeyed my voice. Sometimes we think of blessings as gifts to be enjoyed but when God blesses us, His blessings are intended to overflow to others. In such cases, God's words have to dwell in us richly and be applied to our daily lives.

Col. 3:16 which said "let the word of Christ dwell in you richly in all wisdom." This will lead you, admonish you, establish your heart and make you become worthy of God's vocation of which you have been called. God's divine and indwelling words also lead you into deep meditation. Ever so often one likes to take a little time in their realm to muse. Some may browse the internet, while some may reach for a book, others get earphones and turn the music real low as they muse. Some will take scripture verses the living word or the indwelling word; which will take you deeper and higher in God's realms. The great significance about this is that when you let go and let God stimulate your heart, mind, give you that motivation and engross you into the realms of God; then, you will begin to experience great communications with God. You will receive new revelations, new vision, higher levels in the spirit, your actions and approaches towards God is more sacred as you begin to expand more and more in the works of the Lord. His continuous blessing flows upon your obedience. Acts.9:22 reminded us of how Cornelius sent a delegation, as he was directed by God, to Peter. At this time, God was making a transformation with Peter, of which he had questions, and was a bit hesitant but God made the vision plainer for him. He then moved as God commanded, he acted in obedience and in result gained great blessings on his obedience. Perhaps, the greatest barrier to the spreading of the gospel in the first century was the Jewish-Gentiles conflict. Most of the early believers were Jewish and then it was scandalous even to think of associating with Gentiles but, after Peter received the vision, he afterwards understood that it was his responsibility to go with the messengers into a Gentile home and tell Cornelius the good news of salvation in Jesus Christ.

    Every successful businessman always tries to advertise their company world wide for greater establishment, so should it be with us as Christians. When God begins to bless your obedience, you may not find enough room to store your blessings. So, we should seek ways to establish

God's words. (2 Cor.12) also remind us of Paul's vision of praise. It must be joyous, most glorious and blessed just to be shut in with God. Beholding his beauty and holding communion sweet. No doubt God was taking him to a higher place of praise, or from one glory to the next glory. No wonder the hymnology says 'we shall have a grand time up in heaven, we shall have a grand time up in heaven, have a grand time; walking with the angels, glory hallelujah; we shall have a grand time up in heaven, have a grand time.' Or what a glory that will be when the ransom host we'll see what a hallelujah band when we reach in Beulah's land what a glory that will be. Paul begins to boast in his blessings that came through his obedience. So can we, if we allow God to manifest his will in us as we become willing and obedient to God. Knowing the more you invest in your obedience, the more interest you earn in your blessing; of which the achievement of your reward will lead you to eternal life.

Don't Let Disobedience Stand In The Way Of Your Blessing

We all know that there are consequences to any action we take, what we do can set into motion a series of events that may continue long after we're gone. Unfortunately, when we are making a decision, most of us think only of the immediate consequences. These are often misleading because they are short lived. As we already know that God is no respecter of persons, he is a loving God, a forgiving God and a God of judgment; also he's a consuming fire. You should also know that God's curse towards mankind is a retraction and not as threats. Just put it this way, it is a loving warning about the plain facts of life. Mankind on a whole can be very stubborn and hates to be corrected; also, hates the very fact of being submissive under any circumstances but remember that there are consequences for us to face whether unto disobedience or unto obedience. So then, let it be your responsibility to make wise choices. You sometimes warn your children to stay away from hot stoves and busy streets, in addition, you might even warn them not to walk against the red light; so does God. He warns us to stay away from dangerous actions. The law of the country warns 'do not drink and drive'. If you fail to obey and get caught, or an accident occurs, then you will have to suffer the consequences; whether you like it or not. It is also said that street racers are threats to road users, should they ever be caught or convicted, their cars will be taken away and be destroyed. Hearing these warnings, you probably think society would take precautions or put in action but some choose not to obey, so they pay the penalty. The law of the land is expected to be carried out; not being violated by any means. If not, you pay consequences. How much more God's commands? Think of the many times you have crossed the line, and use the terms "O, well, God understands". Well God does understand. Very well, God does understand that you have violated his law which is disobedience. God is merciful enough to tell us his truth; he is a God of order whose command must be carried out. His truth is also motivated by love not anger; his strong word helps us to avoid the serious consequences that result from neglecting God. There will always be opponents in every aspect of your life and every requirement is a challenge. Everyone is privileged to possess their choice and to every choice there is a reward. Everyone produces positive and negative attitudes; however, if you are desirous of achieving great things in life then of course you will have to stay positive and work hard towards your achievement. As you know, nothing good comes easy. Everyone has a fair share of choice to avoid serious asperity, it is also important for everyone, when making important decisions, that you let your choice be of a high quality.

Your opponent is the devil; he will always try to stand in the way of your blessings and try to let discouragement weigh you down, make you stumble or turn you from the pathway. He will try to turn your heart and thoughts away from God, where in such case you will be damned. Mark16:16 remind us that He that believeth and is baptized shall be saved but he that believeth not shall be damned. A soul that has been damned deserves punishment. What we should realize, regardless of who we are, is that God has given us choices in that we become inexcusable; whether we accept God's words or we reject it. God already knows the danger that lies in disobedience and the success that you can obtain through obedience. God made it plain in his words for us to understand and do them. You should also be aware that blessings come not through favoritism but through obedience, to the word of God, which we shall obtain much blessing and prosperity through his word as we apply them to our daily lives. When there is a blessing on your life, your opponent gets very busy trying to rob you of your access, your rights and privileges. He is a victim to disobedience and, for that cause, God cast him out of heaven. So, in revenge, he will do anything he possibly can to prevent you from obtaining your blessings. Therefore, be extra careful of false teachers, influencers and advisers; be positive with your acceptances and rejections. 1 Pt.5:8 warns us of Satan who is out like a roaring lion ready to attack, so Peter said be sober, be vigilant; because of your adversary, the devil, seeking whom he may devour. Mt.4:2-11 tells us that as Jesus made an end of his forty days and forty nights of fasting, there came the devil to tempt him and deceive him. As you can understand here, the devil used scriptures to convince Jesus to sin. Sometimes, friends or associate will present attractive and convincing reasons for you to believe them. That's why you should try to find bible verses that seem to support their view point, so study the bible carefully, the broader contexts of specific verses, so that you may understand God's principles, and that you will be able to recognize errors. So, when people take verses out of context and have it twisted the way they want, you will know for yourself that it's just a twister.

A person has not shown true obedience if he or she has never had an opportunity to disobey. We read in Deut. 8:2, that God led Israel into the wilderness to humble and test them. God wanted to see whether or not his people would really obey him. We too will be tested because we know that testing will come; we should be alert and ready for it. Remember, your convictions are only strong if they hold up under pressure. The devil, called Satan, tempted Eve in the Garden of Eden, he tempted Jesus in the wilderness and he tempts you on several occasions. Satan is a fallen angel. He is real, not symbolic, and is constantly fighting against those who follow and obey God. Satan's temptations are real and he is already trying to get us to live his way, or our way, rather than God's way. He knows that Jesus will come one day to reign over all creation, so Satan tried to force his hands and get him to declare his kingdom-ship prematurely. If Jesus had given in, his mission on earth to die for our sins and give us the opportunity to have eternal life would have been lost. When temptations seems especially strong, or when you think you can rationalize giving in, just consider whether Satan may be trying to block God's purpose for your life or for someone else's life. Jesus' temptation by the devil showed that Jesus was human and it gives Jesus the opportunity to reaffirm God's plan for his ministry; it also give us an example to follow when we are tempted.

The devil's temptations focused on some crucial areas, physical needs and desire, possessions and power; but Jesus didn't give in. He knows first hand what we are experiencing and he is willing and able to help us in our struggles.

When you're tempted, turn to Jesus for strength. Jesus wasn't tempted when he was in the temple but when he was in the wilderness where he was tired, alone, weak, hungry and vulnerable after forty days and forty nights of fasting and prayer. But, he chose not to use his divine power to satisfy his natural desire for food. Eating is good but the timing was wrong. Jesus was in the wilderness not to eat but to fast. Jesus had given up the unlimited independent use of his divine power in order to experience humanity fully. He wouldn't use his power to change stone in to bread. So then the devil tempts us too when we are vulnerable and are under going physical or emotional stress, lonely, tired and weighing big decisions or focused with uncertainty. But if we, through all circumstances, obey the voice or the word of God the devil can in no wise rob us of our obedience. We shall receive great blessings from the Lord and righteousness from the God of our salvation. Some times our reaction to a moral dilemma often exposes our real motives. Frequently, we are more worried about getting caught than about doing what is right. We should know of a fact that total blessings come from total obedience. To add towards God's words or to subtract from God's words would let it be incomplete. You should also realize that God's word is binding and his blessing is irrevocable; as long as you obey his command. You may find some people who work very hard to make others think that they are smart, the books they carry and the facts they quote are impressive, but Deut. 4:6 tell us that Moses said that a reputation for wisdom comes by obeying God's words. Although, this may not be the most easiest or glamorous way to earn a reputation, it is the most authentic. So don't try to make other think you're intelligent because of what you know, or pretend to know; obeying God's words will give you a far greater reputation because it is not just what you know but what you do that counts.

When we become a victim to disobedience then God's

divine protection is removed from around us. No more fence or edge around us, we become unprotected, we are left open for destruction. Imagine you planted a beautiful vineyard with some precious delicate fruits and vegetables. You fence it around, to protect it from creatures both great and small. It was very attractive to the passers by but, unfortunately, one morning you wake up to find a broken down fence and a destroyed vineyard. No more attraction or beauty. No more lovely comments by passers by because the area is now bear. So it is with us as Christians. Disobedience brings a curse; it robs you of your anointing. You may pretend to be what we are not, because we know the words, but there is no anointing and it's only the anointing will break the yoke. You may sing because you have the voice, but there is no anointing or melody in your singing. You may go to church because someone may enquire about your absence but there is no glory in your appearing and there is no joy or life in your worshipping. God doesn't have part in your disobedience nor does he give glory in it. Does any of this sound like you? See 1 Sam.15:22-24. God rejected Saul as being king because he disobeyed God's command. Saul and his men did not destroy all plundered from the battle as God commanded of them. To break God's law was punishment by death. Josh.7 tells us that breaking the laws of God shows disrespect and disregard for God because it directly violates his command. When we gloss over sin, in order to protect what we have or for material gain, we aren't obeying God's law. Selective obedience is just another form of disobedience. When God said he regretted that he had made Saul king, was he saying he had made a mistake? No, God's comment was an expression of sorrow not an admission of error. (Gen.5:7) An Omniscient God cannot make a mistake; therefore, God did not change his mind but he did change his attitude towards Saul. When Saul changed, his heart was no longer belonging to God, but to his own interests. Saul thought he had won a great victory over the Amalekites but God saw it as a great failure because he had disobeyed him and then lied to Samuel about the results of his battle. Saul may have thought that his lie wouldn't defeat him, or what he did was not wrong, but Saul was deceiving himself. Dishonest people soon begin to believe the lies they construct around themselves then they lose the ability to tell the difference between truth and lies. By believing your own lies, you deceive yourself, alienate yourself from God and you will lose credibility in all your relationships. In the long run, honesty pays off. Understand here, this king was asked to destroy everything but he kept back a part, including the choicest livestock. When Samuel arrived he could hear and see the evidence of Saul's wrong actions but when Saul was confronted Saul said the goods taken were to make a sacrifice to God. This is like saying, in other words, I only stole the cash that I could put a bigger offering in the collection plate. Giving worship and service are meaningless if they flow from a heart that is covering up for sin. If a person's heart is not fully repented, or if he or she didn't really love God, the sacrifice has no real value. In other words, it is hollow and lacking sincerity. Your worship or the ritualism of our worship is empty unless they are performed with an attitude of love and obedience. Being religious, going to church, serving on a committee or even giving to church is not enough if you do not act out of devotion and obedience to God.

A Shelter And A Proctor

A shelter should be a place of protection, or a place of safety, of which the world at large is seeking today. Globally, folks look towards the government of their country as their base support of protection. Therefore, it is the country's responsibility to prepare able men and women who are designated to protecting the country. In today's society, there is not much protection; although, the protectionists tried very hard to control violence and crime but such seems to have no ending because the bible says that the hearts of men are desperately wicked. St. Matt. 24:6 also said "And ye shall hear of wars and rumours of wars: see that ye be not troubled: for all these things must come to pass, but the end is not yet." So, although the government may try very hard to bring down the crime rate, the criminals or oppositions find their different means of discrepancy to suit their bad behavior or their lifestyle. Everyone has to be very extra careful in these days with whom they associate themselves with. There was a time when you could leave your house freely and open up to your neighbors but not anymore. Now you can become a victim of your very neighbors. You could also leave your door unlocked and go to sleep without being fearful, not any more; those days are done gone. Now a days you may try to protect your home or place of business with burglar bars or with some alarm system and every proactive measure you name it, yet you're still not safe. Your true source of security is in Christ. He alone that can pull down all weapons of mass destruction, defeat the purpose of the enemy and declare victory for us unto Christ. Paul declared in 2 Cor.10:4-6 that the weapon of our warfare is not carnal but mighty through God, to the pulling down of strong holds. Do you sometimes feel surrounded by evil and frustrated by the little you can do about it? Don't be shaken, discouraged, weak and faint in your mind but be strong for the name of the Lord, your God, is a strong and a mighty tower, the righteous run into it and are safe. (Pro.18:10) Approximately six years ago the terrorists invaded the United States of America, destroying a lot of loved ones lives. Even today some are still feeling the un-called-for pains and wounds which seem to be freshly done in their minds. Not that the Protectionist wasn't prepared but they were attacked unexpectedly. Had they known that their attackers were upon them then things would have been done differently. The scripture says 'If the watch man of the house had known what time the thief was coming, he would've watched and would not had suffered his house to be broken.' As a matter of fact, the world is very terrified and troubled in their mind. Age is not a factor and profession is not a factor because the mind is unstable and when the mind is unstable then lives are jeopardized. There is peril, hazard and a risk of danger. Not long ago, in April of 2007, there was this young man who was lacking effective emotional control. Being very disturbed distressed and depressed, he walked in to Virginia Tech. University and took the lives of thirty two innocent victims, including students and staff; then turned the weapon upon himself. Just think of the many young lives that were taken without any warning. Many life long dreams disappeared. Is it a shame? There are no answers; no remorse and no respect to the lives of human being anymore. These are the days when you will have to turn to Jesus for the answer because he is the answer for everything that which is known and that which seems to be in the shadows. You can feel the intensity in the atmosphere. Folks of every age everywhere are unsafe; whether in the home, at school, at work or in your car. Therefore, your heart should have that good relationship at all times and make sure you leave the house in good peace with your love ones because there is no guarantee that you will return home safely. So then, before going through your doors don't forget to ask God for his divine protection and as soon as you get in through the doors you should give God thanks as well for his safety and his guidance towards you. Everyday someone is crying because their loved ones have not returned home safely and when you look around you can see your loved ones around that had made it home safely; it makes you feel so blessed. Can you imagine God, after we have been through the testing and the trials, amidst what the devil had put us through? We are safely kept by God; safe in the arms of Jesus. The hymnal says 'O safe to the rock that is higher than I. My soul in its conflicts and sorrows would fly; so sinful, so weary, Thine, Thine would I be; Thou blest rock of ages, I'm hiding in thee." The psalmist David also says in Ps. 61: 4 "I will abide in thy tabernacle forever; I will trust in the covert of thy wings." We will have to find that confidence while we are in God's shelter, feel safe and free in God's providence. Surely he is a very present help in the time of trouble. There will be times when you may feel like all hope is gone and no help is in sight; no help or assistance from anywhere but Job 23:2-10 says sometimes we may find our complaint bitter, and our stroke even heavier than our groaning. Behold, I go forward, but he is not there; and backward, but I cannot perceive him. But he knoweth the way that I take: when he has tried me, I shall come forth as gold. Let us stop feeling sorry for ourselves; arise and shake yourself from the dust and start seeking God's attention. Cry unto your God with the voice of triumph; He will hear you. Don't rush God; just wait for your breakthrough. Ps.69:2-3 declares "I sink in deep mire, where there is no standing: I am come into deep waters, where the floods overflow me. I am weary of my crying: my throat is dried: mine my eyes fail while I wait for my God." Don't give up on yourself because he will not give up on you. He will become your strength giver, your reliance and battle-axe, when it seems as if you are at your weakest point and the devil's warring against your soul. Just remember that there is a rock that you can run to and that rock is Jesus; for on Christ the solid rock I stand, all other ground is sinking sand. Just continue to be firm in your mind and steadfast and true God your strength-giver is coming through for you.

A Refuge Through The Storm

*L*isten to thunder rolling as the lightening flashes across the sky, the heavy rains start to pour, and here comes the boisterous winds blowing. Then you hear the trees falling to the ground, water rising above the grown level, buildings collapsing, properties being destroyed with your loved ones and everything is caving in. Fearful and confused citizens going to and fro seeking a place of refuge, or safety, were they can be sheltered. There are many that are weeping and wailing who can't find their love ones. Refugees are seeking for a way of escape to get to the nearest village, city or country. Some will board the next available plane, boat, or ship going to who knows where because when disaster hits, you are not the same as yesterday but you're mentally disturbed, malfunctioned or disoriented. While many others are left in the ruins, restless nights and hopeless days, no money to spend nor food to eat, no abiding place to stay, one suit on your back; you may have been offered some food but too hungry to say no and too frustrated to eat, the taste of the food may appear as rubber in your mouth. Nothing seems to be passing your throat, down to water seems upsetting. You're too physically, psychologically, emotionally and mentally hurt; never mind the shock and the trauma facing you. You are so sore, tattered and torn inside, with no future in sight. Your eye lids seem very heavy but you dare not shut them due to the many dreadful flashbacks that keep coming back to you. What fear and dread seeing the needy citizens lying on the floor, crying in anguish and pain, with little and no help in sight. The cities and the mountains are suddenly crumbling down and, as a result of the sea, the voices keep screaming out loud for help. It doesn't matter what disaster strikes, or what great danger you think you are facing, God is always on spot ready to take actions. Ps.46:1-10 says "God is our refuge and strength, a very present help in trouble. Therefore will not we fear though the mountains shakes and the swelling thereof." Even if the world ends, we need not fear in the face of utter destruction. For God, who is your refuge, is always there to help provide security and peace. God's power is complete and his ultimate victory is certain. He will not fail to rescue those who love him; he will surely strengthen you, especially in a time when you need him most. The psalmist expressed a quiet confidence in God's ability to save him. It may seem impossible to consider the end of the world without being consumed by fear, but the bible made it very clear that God is our refuge even in the midst of your total destruction. He is not merely a temporary retreat; he is your eternal refuge and can provide strength in any and every circumstances. There may be times when you might be battered and beaten by the boisterous wind, by billows that seem to be tossing high and by the tempestuous raging storms of life. They leave you filled with bitterness and anger as your trials appears one after the next; feeling so desperate because you have no one to turn to. Don't ever feel deserted or lonely because Jesus is the Master of the storm and all billows are subject to obey his voice. Matt.8:24-27 declares "And behold, there arose a great tempest in the sea, insomuch that the ship was covered with the waves: but he was asleep. And his disciples came to him and awoke him, saying, Lord, save us: we perish, And he said unto them, Why are ye fearful, O ye of little faith? Then he arose, and rebuked the winds and the sea; and there was a great calm." You can see that although the disciples had witnessed many miracles, they were panicked in this storm. As experienced sailors, they knew its danger, but what they did not know was that Christ could control the forces of nature. You might sometimes experience a stormy area of your human nature where you feel God can't or won't work. It may seem as if there is no way of escaping it; it may be easy to think that God has lost control and that you are at the mercy of the winds of fate. When we truly understand who God is, we will realize that he controls both the storms of nature and the storms of the troubled heart. Jesus' power that calmed this storm can also help you deal with the problems you face. Jesus is willing to help if you only ask him. We should never discount his power, even in terrible trials. But in reality, God is sovereign. He controls the history of the world as well as your destiny. Just as Jesus calmed the waves, he can calm what ever storm you may face. The disciples panicked because the storm threatened to destroy them all and Jesus seemed to be unaware and unconcerned. There was a physical storm, but storms come in other forms. Think about the storm in your life, the situations that cause you great anxiety. Whatever your difficulties are, you have two options; you can worry and assume that Jesus no longer cares or you can resist fear by putting your trust in him. When you feel like panicking, confess your needs to God and then trust him to care for you. You can be with Christ for many years and yet haven't trusted him enough to bring you through your difficult time because there is fear within you but the only thing that fear can do for you is to destroy your trust and confidence in whom you love. When you love someone, you will trust them. If you love Christ, then trust him because the bible says that perfect love casts away all fear.

Although the disciples lived with Jesus, they underestimated him. They did not see that his power applied to their very own situations. We likewise sometimes underestimated God's power to handle crises in our lives. The disciples did not know enough about Jesus; we cannot make the same mistakes. In whatever situation you may find yourself, be consoled: there is great hope. As Heb. 6:18-19 says "…it is impossible for God to lie, we might have a strong consolation, who have fled for refuge to lay hold upon the hope set before us: Which hope we have as an anchor of the soul, both sure and steadfast, and which entereth into that within the veil." For God embodies all truth; therefore, he cannot lie. God is truth, so you can be secure in his promises. You don't need to wonder if he will change his plans towards you. Your hope is secure and immoveable, anchored in God; just as a ship anchor holds firmly to the seabed. To the seeker who comes to God in faith, God gives an unconditional promise of acceptance. When you ask God, with openness, honesty and sincerity to save you from your sins; he will do it. His truth should give you encouragement, assurance and confidence.

Recovery From The Storm

Feelings are affected by past experiences, which ever aspect it may occur. Whether it may be major, or minor, physical, psychological, emotional, spiritual, or mental; each individual should be dealt with great concern. Some folks, while going through their stage of recuperation or recovery, experience loneliness which causes depression; especially, if there is no family member or relatives to express or relate their feelings to. In Psalm 51, David was very concern about his down fall and was seeking the face of God earnestly in order for God to wash, cleanse, strengthen and bring him back to his rightful place. At the point of his acknowledgement of his mistake, he was very remorseful. He realized that his life was in the hands of the almighty God and he alone could recover him from his major storm. So, with great humility he said 'restore unto me the joy of thy salvation, and uphold me with thy free spirit.' When you are going through your recovery, you may notice that your strength level is very low. You may not have that much joy within you but real joy only comes through Jesus Christ; it's not from a friend or a relative. The bible said that the joy of the Lord is my strength. David likewise said "Make me to hear joy and gladness that the bones which thou has broken may rejoice". You see, when you are weak and shuttered in your mind, you need some reassurance. Like a patient that is recovering from a major surgery and needs to be strengthen with some good tonic, or some multi vitamins, or supplement to regain that perfect health that he or she once had. It not a nice feeling when the muscles and tissues are healing; it's a very sore, painful, and achy procedure but those discomforts are considered as good pain or healing pain. However, no pain indeed seems to be joyful but you continue to look towards better days. In your Christian life, while God is picking up the pieces of your broken heart or of the ruins of your life, he is bringing you back to his righteous standard to revive your soul and make whole again. You must understand that God looks at the heart; he deals with the heart. He circumcises the heart with his words and melts it from solid to liquid (tears); in such cases, it is manageable for God to deal with. So when your heart becomes broken, it is in readiness for repentance. God can step in and bring that heart to recovery. For the sacrifices of God are a broken and a contrite heart, David said in Ps. 51:17, O God thou will not despise. When you begin to play around with God's righteousness, he will hit you right out like one that becomes unconscious. You will have to pay the consequences. There is a saying that's goes like this "you pay double for your trouble!" There is just no easy way of getting back to where you should be; you will have to be submissive as the Lord has His way. When you become unsuitable for God's intended purpose, he will have to wash you, cleanse you, mold you and make you into his own likeness; into an acceptable and unblemished work. God shall comfort your heart, if you seek him and listen to his voice. Focus on him who is the rock of your salvation, to him who has pulled you from the ruins, to him who had carried you on eagle's wings through the boisterous storm, the one who gives you joy and gladness and the voice of melody throughout your aching pains and sorrows. Although you had been a victim through the raging storm, God allowed you to survive. Being homeless and without shelter is when you leave God's divine presence; you are on your own without protection, traveling in an uncertain direction and you're exposed to danger. Being weak, hungry, and thirsty is when you refuse to accept the word of God; rebelliousness occupies the mind in such a way that God's divine word cannot be rooted within the heart to give you life. The word of God said in John 6:35 "And Jesus said unto them, I am the bread of life: he that cometh to me shall never hunger; and he that believeth on me shall never thirst. Verse 51 states, "I am the living bread which came down from heaven: If any man eat of this bread, he shall live for ever: and the bread that I will give is my flesh, which I will give for the life of the world." Jesus offered himself as spiritual bread from heaven; it should dwell in you richly and satisfy you completely. This also leads you to eternal life in Jesus Christ.

When disaster strikes, it can leave you sad, broken, ruined, depressed, oppressed, separated, even to the point of death. But when disaster strikes, don't be panic, just remember that God is the one that both strengthens and weaken the wind, and also rides upon the wings of the winds. Ps.37:22-25 said "For such as be blessed of him shall inherit the earth; and they that be cursed of him shall be cut off. The steps of a good man are ordered by the Lord: and he delighteth in his way. Though he fall, he shall not be utterly cast down: for the Lord upholdeth him with his hand. I have been young, and now am old; yet have I not seen the righteous forsaken, nor his seed begging bread."

This is Part Two

How Much Do You Love Him

How delightful it is for Pilots to put confidence in their planes, Commuters place confidence in trains, or cars, or buses. Each day we should have great pleasure in putting our confidence in someone or something. If you are willing to trust a plane or a car to get you to your destination, are you willing to trust God to guide you here on earth to your final destination?

How futile it is to trust anything, or any one more than God, who can you rely on or put your trust in? In today's society, there are many invaders, conspirators, hostages, and pornographies that surround us in our homes, on the internet, on the streets, at schools, in the hospitals. O! How terrifying? These attitudes minimize trust in human being and it also brings down moral lifestyle and integrity. Ps.26:1 says "Judge me, O Lord; for I have walked in mine integrity, I have also trust the Lord; therefore I shall not slide." So then, it is questionable, should I stay away from society or should I isolate myself? No. Although the unpredictable behavior is in the atmosphere, you will have to trust God, who is able to monitor each move that you make; for he alone is aware of the known and the unknown.

Trust God For Deliverance Makes A Difference

We can never avoid strife in the world around us, but with God we know there is always perfect peace and safety. Even when life seems to be empty and hopeless, there is an arm that always brings sweet deliverance, strength and victory; strength for today and great hope for tomorrow even in the worse turmoil. If you devote your life to God your whole attitude will be steady and stable, because it is supported by the unchanging love of God and his strong and mighty power. So then with great confidence you can say, you are not shaken by surrounding chaos. Ph.4:6-7 said, we should not be anxious for nothing, but in every thing by prayer and supplication with thanksgiving let your requests be made known unto God. And the peace of God, which passes all understanding, will keep your hearts and minds through Christ Jesus. God is such an awesome God; just imagine never being anxious about any situation, no matter how terrible it may seems to you. God said be not anxious because he has already taken care of the situation. But as humans, we seem to have that temper tantrum or act as that crying baby that will never stop crying, until they are pampered, pacified or that bottle is in the mouth. But don't wait for that bottle or the pacifier to be place in your mouth, or to be pampered, to know that God is there. He said he will never leave you comfortless and you will have to believe it. God is trying to let you understand that he was your yesterday, he is your today, and he will also be your tomorrow. He is your entire future. It might seem impossible, but your God is in control at all times. You will experience worries on the job, in your home or at school but Paul's advice to us is that we turn our worries in to prayer. Do you want to become worriless? Then fast and pray more. When you start to worry stop and pray. When you wake up in the middle of the night and you can't sleep, then its time for you to pray. Have you ever been sleeping and some unwelcome spirit comes to attack you trying to silence you in your sleep and you are struggling to say "Jesus"; however, the word "Jesus" can't even comes out? Yet when Jesus releases his holy anointing, and the Holy Spirit takes charge, then all devils will have to flee at the mention of his name. Some forces are very determined, or persistent, so you will have to be filled up with God's power and be ready to attack. This is a good suggestion for all Christians, you should practice to wake up in the night and pray. If you have not been doing so, then you should start doing so. If you practice it, it will become a habitual thing for you, a great midnight activity. Indeed it will be a great sacrifice for you to make but it will pay off in the long run. You see, God loves to communicate with mankind, as he usually did with Adam in the cool of the day, see Gen. 3:9. In the stillness of the midnight, when the house seems to be quiet and everyone is sound asleep, it is the best time to steal away to God. As you get into your closet and invite God presence into your chamber, don't be afraid, but feel free to strip yourself before him. Start pouring out to him and he will surely download into your system. God's desire is to have fellowship with you. The hymnology said "I come to the garden alone, while the dew is still on the roses, and the voice I hear, falling on my ear the son of God discloses. And he walks with me and he talks with me and he tells me I am his own; and the joy we share as we tarry there, none other has ever known." You shouldn't be afraid to be in the presence of God, as Adam and Eve were afraid when they heard him approaching the garden. God wanted to be with them but because of their sins they were afraid to show themselves. Sin had broken their close relationship with God, just as it has broken ours many times. But Jesus Christ opened the way for us to renew our fellowship with him; see him as the lover of your life. God longs to be with you, to remind you that you are his own, to commune with you and to unfold his mystery in to your spirit. He who offers to you his unconditional love; regardless of your faults, God can remove that dread. Maybe its time to own your wrong attitudes and actions and apologize to God. Physically, God allows the immune system to protect the body from disease and infection, which sometimes the body produces substances that cause the body to attack itself. Micro organisms, bacteria, viruses and other germs in the environment can lead to an infection, so then the body depends on the immune system for its protection. Sometimes, your mind is the greatest problem because it is filled with many doubts and fears. It can be easily broken down with sin but God, who is the divine controller and the protector of your spiritual holism, can protect the mind from every sinful disease and thought that will germinate in the heart to infect the mind soul and spirit. God is able to release the blockage, unclog the mind and allow you to have that continuous open communication with him where you will experience a deep settled peace with him. Jn.14:27 tells us that true peace is not found in positive thinking, in absence of conflict, or in good feeling, but it comes from knowing that God is in charge. It about time you be aware of the fact that your citizenship in Christ's Kingdom is sure, your destiny is set, and you can have victory over sin. Let God peace guard your heart against anxiety, then you shall be delivered at all times. When Paul said in Ep. 6:10, be strong in the Lord and in the power of his might, you have to guard yourself because it is a time of warfare. Your mind has to be fully clothed with the word of God and, as true soldiers, be fit, be ready and be prepared to fight your foes. With that great initiative, you will be a winner all the time. Knowing that whatever you put into your mind determines what comes out in your words and actions. Let us program our minds with thoughts that are noble, right, pure, lovely, just, virtuous, praise worthy and also of good report. Do you sometimes have trouble or problems with impure thoughts and daydreams? Then examine what you are putting into your mind through television, books, conversations, movies, clubs, and magazines. You can replace harmful input with wholesome material and, above all, read God's powerful words. Pray and ask God to help you focus your mind with his powerful Holy Ghost, which will deliver you from all evil.

Do You Trust Him To Be Your Friend

*L*oneliness is everywhere. Many people feel cut off and alienated from others; being in a crowd just makes people more aware of their isolation. We all need friends who will stick close to us, listen to us, care for us and offer help when it is needed. In good times and bad times, it is better to have one such friend than dozens of superficial acquaintances. Instead of wishing that you could find a true friend, you should seek to become one. There are people who need your friendship, Ask God to reveal them to you, and then take the challenge of being a true friend. I am not the least jealous of the writer as he penned these words "A friend of Jesus, oh what bliss that one as weak as I; should ever have a friend like this to lead me to the sky". Still writing he said "Friendship with Jesus, fellowship divine; oh what blessed sweet communion, Jesus is a friend of mine". When seeking to find friends, make sure your life is up to standard. Be a good mentor, not a slanderer, a good communicator, not a bad influence, and with integrity. Integrity is far more valuable than wealth; although, most people don't act as if they believe this. They are afraid of not getting everything they want; they will pay any price to increase their wealth, even if it means cheating on their taxes, stealing from stores and employers, withholding tithes and offering and refusing to give. But when we both know and love God, we will realize that a lower standard of living, or even poverty, is a small price to pay for personal integrity. Do your actions show that you sacrifice your integrity to increase your wealth? Ask yourself the question, what changes do you need to make in order to get your priorities straight? Jesus did make his priority straight when he gave his life as a ransom for us. See Jn.15:13 say "Greater love has no man than this to lay down his life for his friends". When you allow God to be your friend, all your loneliness will be over. He is a God that will be there for you whatever it takes. On the mountain peak or down in the valley low, in sickness or in health, in sad times or in the good times, if your house is that mansion on the hilltop or a cottage or tent by the wayside. Whether you live from pay cheque to pay cheque or have millions in the bank, you don't have to impress God to be a friend of his. He will come to your level no matter what. One day, one of my friends was trying to impress me by telling me that she has this large x amount of shoes, and I only have a few x amounts of shoes I let her talk because she could only see the visible. I then said to her 'you give God thanks for your huge amount of shoes, and let me give God thanks for my few x amount of shoes, because I can only were one pair at a time and so do you'. Let us not try to impress others that they may feel less fortunate, less important or make them feel embarrassed but give thanks to

God who has provided for you. Continue to trust him; he is that friend that sticks closer than a brother. The bible tells us about a certain Prophet by the name of Elijah, (1 Kg.19:4-15) who found himself in the wilderness. He was very lonely, he thought he was forgotten and had no more hope. He complained that all the Prophets were dead, that he was left alone and his enemy required his life; so he made a request for God to take his life. But in his time of despair, God sent his angel to comfort and admonish him, feed him with food and drink to strengthen him for his journey and let him know that he's not alone for there were seven thousand left in Israel which had not bowed their knees unto Baal. So there will be times when you will feel hopeless, friendless, lonesome, hungry, and weak, like no body cares and you might ask the question of yourself "Lord why? What have I done?" "Where have I gone wrong?" Or "where are you Lord?" "Lord do you really care?" But whatever it might be, don't give up or give in and don't ever quit. Just trust God, he is the only true friend. Help is already on the way, God has dispatched his angels round about you. Just at the point of you giving up, God is coming through for you; to encamp, to comfort and strengthen you. He is about to release your breakthrough. Oh isn't God wonderful! What a precious friend is he.

Do You Trust Him To Be Your Lawyer

As you may already be aware of the fact that there are various types of lawyers such as they that conduct lawsuits for clients, or advises you as to legal rights and obligations in other matters, the Bible makes reference to different types of laws as noted in the Holy Scripture:

Ceremonial Law: This kind of law relates specifically to Israel's Worship (Lev.1:1-13). Its primary purpose was to Point forward to Jesus Christ; therefore, these laws Were no longer necessary after Jesus' death and Resurrection. While we are no longer bound by Ceremonial laws, the principles behind them to Worship and love a Holy God still apply. The Jewish Christians often accused the Gentile Christians of violating ceremonial laws.

Civil Law: This type of law dictated Israel's daily Living (De.24:10-11) because modern Society and culture are so radical. But The principles behind the commands should guide our conduct. There was a time when Paul ask Christians to follow some of these laws not Because they had to, but in order to promote unity.

Moral Law: This sort of law is the direct command of God: For example The Ten Commandments (Ex.20:1-17). It requires strict obedience. It reveals the nature and will of God and it still applies to us today. We are to obey the moral laws, not only to obtain salvation but to live in ways well pleasing to God.

Jesus Christ is the only one that can plead your case for you, for eternal life, which he did for us when he was nailed to the cross. The bible said that we all have sinned and come short of the glory of God (Ro.3:20-24). After all the bad news about our sinfulness and condemnation, Paul gives the wonderful news. There is a way to be declared not guilty and that's by trusting Jesus Christ to take away your sins. Trusting means putting your confidence in Christ to forgive your sins; that you may make things right with God and to empower you to live the way he taught you. God's solution is available to all of us; Regardless of your background or past behavior. Some sins may seem bigger than others, because their obvious consequences are more serious. Murder, for example may seem to us way worse than lies, but this does not mean that because we do lesser sins we deserve eternal life. We will be accountable for all sin. All sins make us sinners. All sins cut us off from the Almighty God. All sins leads to death because it disqualifies us from living with God; regardless, of how great or how small it seems. So please don't minimize, or under rate, little and big sins; they all separate us from God. But there is one good thing about this, they all can be forgiven.

Thanks be to Jesus Christ for justification through is death, Paul said in one of his teaching (Rom.5:1) being justified with Christ we shall have peace with God. Being 'justified' means to be declared not guilty. When God who is your judge declared you not guilty, all charges are dropped, or your sin has been removed from your record. Really, it is as if you had never been sin. When God forgives your sins, your record is wiped clean. From his perspective, you're free for his eternal kingdom.

Some time ago there was an incident between me and one of my neighbors, who was residing one level below me. She has always been complaining about un-pleasant sound she has been encountering with very late at night to early morning between 1: am. -5: am. which unable her to rest comfortably due to the sound. At this time she was trying to accuse me with an allegation that the sound was coming from my suit with an assumption that my children has been up during the nights playing ball. This was really senseless to me. We both appeared before an Adjudicator who had the matter settled and dismissed her case. Justice was been served because God who is the greater Adjudicator, whose eyes are in every secret places, whose omnipresent is every where beholding both good and bad, who is the justifier and he shall bring every work into judgment. He is the greater judge who interacts with the mind of humanity and shall bring all things in to justice.

Sometimes you may live in a certain area, surrounding or environment where you do not feel welcome, people will try their endeavor best or do anything to get rid of you; even if it means making up an untrue story. "Didn't they do that to Jesus? you bet they did" But, when the devil thinks he is up to some thing big, God can bring him down to nothing because when the devil makes his plans, God has a way of canceling them. For when God is for you, no one can be against you. I encourage you to trust God, who is capable of settling all matters. Ro.3:25 tell us that Christ is our propitiation, our sacrifice of atonement. In other words, he died in your place for your sins. God is justifiably angry at sinners because they have rebelled against him and cut themselves off from his life giving power. But God declares Christ's death, because He died in our place, as having paid the penalty of death for our sin. Glory be to God! His sacrifice brings pardon, deliverance and freedom.

Just How Much Do You Really Trust God

I trust God who has brought down every high place and elevated every waste places. I trust him who has the power to subdue all enemies under feet, who alone can make the impossible to be possible. He who turned the water into wine and caused the lame to walk again; the mighty God, the strong tower, that great rock, in him do I put my trust. The Psalmist David noted in Ps.61:4 I will abide in thy tabernacle for ever: I will trust in the covert of thy wings. David expresses a fundamental truth by which every believer should live. That in time of trouble, or opposition from the enemies you can turn to God as your ultimate refuge and deliverer. Every believer who trust in God should be able to say I will not allow trouble, crisis, or suffering to shake my confidence in God. Because in Him is my strength and my salvation. Isaiah 12:2 also said, Behold God is my salvation, I will trust and not be afraid for the Lord Jehovah is my strength, and my song, He also become my salvation

This is a true testimony of how I trusted God, by faith, and he came through for me. I also want you to know that what God had done for me he can do the same for you, if you trust him.

I had worked for a certain company for approximately fourteen plus years. Unfortunately, the company downsized and my department was completely closed. I was laid off indefinitely.

I then decided to upgrade my skills, which I think was a good thought. One fine Friday afternoon on my way from school, I stopped by the mailbox only to discover an eviction notice; which had been delayed somewhere for approximately two weeks according to the date appearing on the document. However, from the time it was sent to the time we received it, we only had three more days to take action. Nothing could be done, naturally, because it was already 6pm Friday evening and we are supposing to leave the building by 12 noon Monday.

Referring to the story mentioned on the previous pages concerning the noise issue, the defeated neighbor wasn't satisfied with having lost her case (but that's ok because the devil hates being defeated but he has to accept the fact that he is a defeated foe), optimistically she sought the landlord's attention who went and filed an eviction notice.

The landlord stated that he needed the space to accommodate some family members of his. On this note my husband was very confused and being the man of the house he was concerned about where to house his wife and children in the space of three days, as any caring husband would be concerned. I said to my husband 'don't worry yourself, just be strong, sometimes things have to get worst before it can get better. I am not going to put up a fight against God because God knows what he is doing and he must have somewhere better in store for us.'

There was absolutely no reason for me to be worried or troubled in mind because I take God at his word. If God is in control and he is about to do a work you will just have to allow him to have his way. In Mk. 11:22-24, the bible says "Have faith in God. For verily I say unto you, that whosoever shall say unto this mountain, be thou removed, and be thou cast into the sea; and shall not doubt in his heart, but shall believe that those things which he saith shall come to pass; he shall have whatsoever he saith. Therefore I say unto you, what things so ever ye desire, when ye pray, believe that ye receive them, and ye shall have them."

I declared God's divine word upon my situation and allow faith to take hold of the work. In Gen.28:18 said. And Jacob rose up early the morning, and took the stone that he had put for his pillows, and set it up for a pillar, and poured oil upon the top of it. So did I took my Olive oil, and poured it upon the notice and then anointed my entire family with the Olive oil, and also my main door, and side door. The bible says in Ex.12:7-13 when I see the blood I will pass over you. I then turn to my heavenly Father, my provider, the God of Isaac, the God of Abraham, the God Shadrach, Meshach, and Abednego, the God of all gods, my rock, my refuge, my safe hiding place and prayed this prayer "Hear me now God, in my hands is this notice for us to evacuate this building in a few days, every governmental office is now closed at this time. There is no access to locate any one until Monday morning at 8am. But here you are, the highest Authority, intervene at this time. Release Michael, your Archangel, and allow him to stand by the front door with flaming sword. Give your angels charge to encamp around this building. Your word told me that the angels of the Lord encampeth round about them that fear you. We will leave this place but not in three days but when you give us the order to do so. We trust you now God to work upon this petition."

I went to my bed and in the middle of the night I had a vision. I saw a bright light, it shone as bright as the sun, being carried by the hand of a man (of which I could only see from the waist going down to his feet). The light shone through my window on my face (a fervent heat was coming from the light), then the light went around to my front door and stood there. I said to my husband, the light is at the door let's go and worship, but behold it was a vision. No sooner I awoke from my sleep realizing it was a vision, I got up went to the door and worshipped the Lord. I believed that God was letting me know that my prayer was answered and that His divine protection that I have asked for was granted. And I know without a doubt that every thing was going to be alright. We had a friend who is a real-estate agent and in the morning we got in touch with her. She came and gave us some good advice. She acted very promptly, showed great expertise in the setting up of various appointments for the viewing of properties. Prior to this incident we had no intention of embarking in a real - estate investment, so we were currently unprepared for such task. Neither were we intended to settle for another unit but to excel as God would have us do. Who can fathom God, or who can understand the way he does works? Surely the righteous shall give thanks unto his name: the upright shall dwell in his presence.

On Sunday morning during devotion, we prayed as we were led by God, in addition we also seek for God's divine leading and direction that he will choose for us the right accommodation, neighborhood, and environmental surrounding. After devotion, I hastily went to the kitchen to make breakfast for the family. At the same time trying to manage time, in order to be on time for Sunday School. However this great amazing thing happens, while I was at the stove I heard a voice speak to me saying 'turn off the stove, go and pray.' I smiled and said to myself that I just finish praying. At this time I was thinking to myself that the first prayer was good enough, but here God was telling me to seek him some more. That morning I went to eight different corners of that apartment and prayed to the almighty God I just did what he had required of me. As said Lam.3:24-25 The Lord is my portion, saith my soul therefore will I hope in Him. The Lord is good unto them that wait for him, to the soul that seeketh him. Let me also mingle the words of this writer, 'Gods' voice makes a difference. When he speaks he relieves my troubled mind. It's the only voice I hear that makes a difference and I follow it one day at a time.'

We didn't let this situation be a threat to our daily lifestyle as we continued with our regular activities. In the weeks that follow we went about viewing
several properties. And was successful in making a choice with the real-estate agent and myself. My husband was away on business, but soon as he returned home he made the final decision and put an offer in which was accepted. We were very grateful to God; we do worship him for his goodness. From the moment my eyes behold the property I claimed it in Jesus' name and with such seal I knew it would be ours. During this period we were living out our last month rent. And things were really looking up for us. The only thing that would've seems to be a problem is a place of accommodation for the period of six weeks, as we patiently wait with much anticipatory and great excitement with the expectancy of our relocation which would be available in approximately two months. Our main focus was towards our six weeks living accommodation and our up coming closing.

During this crucial time my mind seems to have been

on a wild chase as expected of any human being so I decided to weigh the condition and let God made the choice. In the meds of my mixed thoughts I went to church with a friend of mine and having listening to the preacher's topic "God is going to make you laugh" based on Sarah's miracle when the angel told her she was going to bear a child (son) Gen. 18:12-15. There was a Meeting at my home church also that I had attended and the word was "receive your miracle). The preacher spoke out "there is a miracle here for a sister come and receive it now" I knew without a doubt that it was me so without any hesitant I went and receive my miracle. When I matched both preacher's message to gather I realize that the spoken words was a conformation to my situation. Surely God does work in mysterious ways and his wonders to perform he plant his foot steps up on the sea and he rides up on the storm as said the song writer. My living accommodation now became very optional. What a God? Sometimes we truly fail to remember that the Holy Scripture declares unto us that the cattle upon a thousand hills are his and that he also supplies our need accordingly to his riches in glory. (Heb.11:1) encourages, that faith is the substance of things hope for the evidence of things not seen. Also (Ro.8:24-25) says "For we are saved by hope: but hope that is seen is not hope: for what a man seeth, why doth he yet hope for? But if we hope for that we see not, then do we with patience wait for it".

It was now time for us to move so we moved and resided with one of my sister and (best friend) for a period of six weeks. Every day had seems brighter than the day before. No wonder Jeremiah said "Morning by morning new mercies I see all that I've needed thy hands hath provided great is thy faithfulness Lord unto me". It is our nature sometimes to make our own plans and then seek Gods blessings on them. Instead we should first seek God who will allow us to make the right decisions who will also counsel us and give us wisdom. God loves his children with an everlasting love, such love that cannot fade away yet he does not exempt us from the day to day circumstances of live as mothers that cares about their toddlers and pay close attention as they try to walk but unfortunately they all struggle and fall before they can walk independently. So believers and unbelievers will experience pain, trouble and failure a times. It is very important that all believers should have confident in he whom they believe in that God will not for get them don't matter what the circumstances may be.

Coming to the closer of a real-estate investment always been a challenge, never mind how well organize things look from your prospective. The other end never seems to be organized, there are always some unfinished work, which leave you with some of the last minutes running around which also can make you very frustrated, and of course we weren't exempted.

Sometimes God will showed up unaware and invade your territory, widen your borders letting you know it time to move on. 1Sam.1:4-5 said, And when the time was that Elkanah offered, he gave to Pe-nin-nah his wife, and to all her sons and her daughters, portions: But unto Hannah he gave a worthy portion; for he love Hannah: but the Lord had shut up her womb. But Hannah did not settle for just a worthy portion but prayed her way through and God delivered her by removing her reproach and fill her heart with joy and gladness and her mouth with praise .Although things were done spitefully, and maliciously. But here God came through for us and lavishly install us formally accordingly to his will.

You may find yourself in this or similar situation; it

may be a house, a car or something else but whatever it may be, just remember that God can and that he will make a way when there does not seem to be a way. When your own turns you down, its time to know that it is God's job. It is natural for children to trust their parents, even though parents some times fail to keep their promise, but your heavenly father never make promises he won't keep. However, his plan may take longer than you've expected; however let us not act as impatient children but wait for God's will to be unfolded. Place your confidence in God's goodness and power. When I saw the light pass by and shone on me then went around to my door and stood there, I knew immediately not to fear for God was in the midst of us. No darkness, devil or disappointment could be able to stand in our way. Is.58:8-9 said, "Then shall thy light break forth as the morning, and thine health shall spring forth speedily; and thy righteousness shall go before thee; the glory of the Lord shall be thy rereward. Then shall thou call, and the Lord shall answer; thou shall cry, and he shall say, here I am."; Pro.3:5-6 tell us that we should "trust in the Lord with all thine heart; and lean not unto thine own understanding. In all thy ways acknowledge him, and he shall direct thy paths." Sometimes you may feel that you can't even trust your very own self, but God is the better judge of what you should trust completely in. Every choice you make you should not be wise only in your own eyes, but always be willing to listen and also willing to be corrected by God. Bring your decision to God in prayer and use the bible as your guide because it is indeed your compass. Follow God's leading he will make your path straight by both guiding and protecting you, for only God knows what best for you.

The Healer Of Every Sickness

We are aware of the fact that there are sicknesses everywhere, and there are several different types of epidemics and diseases that are common among human beings. There are some epidemics that are very contagious, so people that are affected with contagious disease would become indispose, isolated or be quarantined. There are some diseases that are curable, and some diseases that are incurable. There are sicknesses that even some health specialist can't even figure out, but now a days the health care system will take every desperate measure to do researches to find the provincial, and the cure. There are also other ways for disease prevention such as immunization, which can prevent many infectious diseases. In early bible days one of the main highly contagious diseases was leprosy, which is a severe skin disease that was greatly feared. This disease can slowly ruin your body and in most cases was fatal.

Lepers were separated from family and friends so all those who had been diagnosed would have been quarantined. Only the Priest was able to give the prognoses because they made the decision when the person was truly cured.

To be healthy is very valuable and to keep healthy is even much more valuable; therefore, every one that loves a healthy lifestyle or loves to stay fit should eat healthy, sleep well, and visit the physician on a regular basis. However, there are some sicknesses that can attack you suddenly and can cut you off immediately. Also there are acute sicknesses that can attack you suddenly, but only stay for a short time. So then, because of sickness and diseases, health care workers are always on the go. They work twenty four seven and even with such great interest and potential sicknesses and diseases are still on the rise.

I indeed give man much, much credit to the health care system that finds great pleasure in seeking out ways to restore the health and well being of their fellow men. I truly think it must be beyond imagination how physician feels when they try to restore one back to life, even by resuscitation, and the system fails. It must be terrifying; however, man can only do so much. So then if any sickness should rise up on you and the physician can not cure you, please do not put the blame on them (especially when they have gone to the very extreme to use up every method in the book) because they cannot go beyond the faculty of their learning. There will always be health issues; there will also be diagnosis, prognosis and puzzling health questions.

But there is one that is above all others how wonderful is he. He is the great physician, the mighty God. He is the one that formed mankind in his own image. He who created the Cerebrum which is said to be the largest part of the brain, which is also the center of all thought and intelligence. He is also the author of the Cerebral Cortex that is also said to control the highest functions of the brain which includes your reasoning, your memory, your consciousness, your speech, your movement and also your five senses. Without these functions of the brain your health is poor. He who structured the body and fitly joined them together, caused it to function in its rightful manner; to him be all praise, honor, glory, majesty and power. So if you feel your body not responding the way it should be, you should feel free to get in touch with your maker. When you seek him, even if you have to seek medical help, he knows you better than any one else and will allow the doctor to come up with the right diagnosis as well as give you the right prescription for your complaint.

He Can Make You Whole

The bible tells me in St. Mk. 5:25-34 of a certain woman who had an issue of blood for twelve long years. She had visited many physicians, she had spent all the money she had on her sickness but unfortunately they couldn't cure her of her disease. It so happens that Jesus was passing by with a large crowd following him and she knew that Jesus could heal her. She pressed through the crowd with great faith believing that if she could only touch the hem of his garment she would be healed. She pressed her way through and touched the hem of Jesus' garment and immediately she was made whole of her disease. I can imagine how blessed she must have felt, that her disease had been cured, and the only thing it cost her was faith. After spending all that she had on the physicians and remained uncured but the moment she reached out to Jesus, by faith, she was healed. Jesus responded to her situation by letting her know that her faith had made her whole. This woman's faith and experience has left the world a legacy. I am sure she is not the only one that had been sick and had tried everything possible but their condition turned out to be the same or even worse before they decided to try Jesus to have Jesus come through for them. What about that testimony? Did you forget to tell others of his goodness or of his healing power? When he heals you, you should tell some one else that may be going through the same thing you have been through or even worse and your testimony can come through for them; it will come alive unto them. Are you guilty of receiving an invitation to a church service and for some reason you slight that invitation (maybe because of fear, pride or for whatever reason)? Yet, when sickness get a hold of your body where it seems like you just won't get well and every breath that you take is a challenge, where it seems like you have fallen between the rock and the hard place that you send a request to the pastor of the church for you to be prayed for; as you negotiate with God saying that if he would only touch you or heal you of your sickness or your disease that you would serve him for the rest of your life? However, after he has healed you, as soon as your health has been restored, you forget all about what you have been through and the promise you have made unto the Lord. Or have promised him that if he heal you, you will attend church on a more regular basis, promise to be at every fasting service, every prayer service, every bible education assembling, be early for Sunday school, will do your tithing and you will love and serve him better? What about the promises you had made, are you keeping up with them? Do you feel guilty about this? Think about it seriously and live by your promise. What if Jesus didn't help you? What if he didn't come down to your level? What if he didn't cure you of your depression? What If he didn't heal your confused mind? What if he didn't come through for your children or provide you with that job? Maybe you would have been worse off or have been cut off. Many people are so confused at times with medication and prayer, as they would be confused with herbal medicine and prescription medicine. For example, you may be experiencing a headache or cramps which may be very severe so you pray for God to take the pain away but the moment you finish praying you reached for the painkiller. In the next few minutes, you start feeling better or you're back to normal and now you are wondering if it the painkiller or the prayer that worked. Don't get confused, the reason is, you didn't allow faith through prayer to have its full course; neither did you allow the painkiller to work independently. If you are going to use the painkiller then use the painkiller for that is where your faith is. If you are going to pray, just pray believing through faith that Jesus is going to heal you and let faith have its perfect way. In such cases, you'll be able to identify what source took care of your problem. Also, you may want to take that medication and pray by faith that God will allow his healing virtue to work through that medication so that your condition may be cured.

I have come to realize that God is not an ordinary God and I have also acknowledged that he is more than just an extraordinary God. There is just no word to describe him. He who is the beginning and the ending, the Alpha and the Omega, the first and the last (Rev.1:11). He is the only God that heals and deliver, he alone that can work on every major case and also the minors. The cases that doctors can't manage, you can turn it over to him. The question was asked is there any thing too hard for God? (Gen.18:14) Of course not!

I remember at the age of fourteen I was diagnosed with eczema – a disease of the skin which causes from excess dryness of the skin, it can be very itchy, very irritating and uncomfortable. And appears at the sensitive areas of the body. During my encounter I experience much discomfort which could be possible prevented just by letting my parents aware of my condition. But becoming adolescence and experiencing the psychological maturity. Embarrassment stepped in and became a barrier which causes me not to share my hurt with my parents' while it was yet controllable. And of course, in those days you would've withheld back lot of stuff on the inside of which you would rather feel free to share with your peers. Folks to day don't have to be embarrassed or feel shameful to disclose a situation that is bothersome or unpleasant because that embarrassment cycle has been diminished or broken. the highlight of the educational system as removed such demarcation. So young folks, feel free to download your situation to your parents don't let embarrassment prevent you from sharing a healthy lifestyle because they know best. I endure to the point where my condition gets to the core and was quite unbearable. I brought it to my parents' attention. When they discovered my sickness they sought the doctor's immediate attention. At this point inflammation oozing occurred. Trust me, it was very uncomfortable and even just reviewing it over within my mind makes me shivers. Every other morning on my way to school I had to stop by the hospital to have them dressed my wounds. The nurses were very empathic which made me courageous in anticipating better days. There were times I thought of Job, whose whole body was covered off with sores, nothing to compare with what I was experiencing. So I strengthen myself knowing that I wasn't all that bad as I could wear my clothes but Job was not able to be clothed. For four consecutive years, I had been visiting the doctor and while I was on the medication the condition seem to be a bit better; but, as soon as the medication was finish, the condition remained the same and some times worse because some of the medication made it more irritable. Upon one of my visits to the doctor, I think that she was tired of seeing me and so was I tired of seeing her for none of her medications seems to be working out for me, the doctor asked my mother, that prescription I filled for your daughter didn't work? Well this condition doesn't really get better, look between my fingers, she showed us, I have had the same thing from I was a child and it hasn't been better. At this point, she was trying to say to us that there was nothing more she could have done for me. Now I realized that there was really nothing she could have done for me because it wasn't really the doctor's job.

Now the Lord had opened a channel for me to travel to Canada and my condition was still there. So, I refused to travel to Canada in such a condition because God is in all complete. I started reasoning with the Lord. I said "Lord I asked you to work a miracle for me to go to Canada (this miracle will be explained to you in another chapter) is this the way you are going to send me?" Ps.84:11 said, for the Lord God is a sun and shield: the Lord will give grace and glory: no good thing will he withhold from them that walk uprightly. The song writer also indicate that, You can have a little talk with Jesus, You can tell him all about your trouble he will hear your fainting cry and he will answer by and by when you feel a little fire is burning you can know a little prayer wheel turning you can have a little talk with Jesus make it right. While I was there seeking God for his cleansing touch, and healing virtue I heard a voice say to me 'go on seven days of fasting starting tomorrow'. I obeyed the voice and I went on seven days of fasting. When I went to church the Sunday, at the ending of the week of the fasting, I was sitting at my usual spot on the choir when the Holy Ghost power started moving in a mighty way. When an anointed Holy Ghost filled, tongue talking, Evangelist, woman of God came and anointed my chest and my breasts in the name of Jesus Christ (just the area where the symptoms were). Isn't God good? From that day until this day my disease has be cured by Jesus Christ. Some times when I think of God goodness towards me, I just want to scream, jump high and holler aloud. For who am I that he should be so gracious towards me? All the ointments, the creams, the washes, the home remedies could not had cured my disease because Jesus was the answer for my problem. This had advanced my level of faith. You don't have to wait until the doctor gets tired of seeing you and you don't have to wait for them to tell you that there is nothing else they can do for you or to wait the many years I had waited to prove that the job wasn't for the doctor. But, whenever there is a problem, first seek God. He is the answer for every situation and the solution for every problem. When I asked God to wash me, I didn't want anything to prevent God's healing virtue towards me; for sometimes when you think you are righteous before God, you are more in an undone state. You may think you are sweetly saved but just take a self examination then you would see how undone you are before God. You are only filthy rags. It doesn't matter how far you get in sin, God can heal your sin sick heart, change your heart, change your thoughts, give you a clear mind and a clear conscience. When God fixes you up, then you are well empowered. Is.6:5-8 relates to us, when Isaiah sought the Lord and seeing and listening to the praise of angels, how he realized how unclean he was before God. He recognized that he of himself had no hope of measuring up to God's standard of holiness. Maybe in the time of your circumstances you thought that a life for you with the Lord was not good any more. Maybe you were enticed by your friends or have been influenced by the every day lifestyle – to be more like them than more like God; but arise and speak life and power into your spirit. Strengthen yourself and let God use you. You are employed by God. The prophet's lofty view of God gives us a sense of God's greatness, mystery and power. Recognizing his sinfulness before God encourages us to confess our sins. His picture of forgiveness reminds us that we too are forgiven. Just think of God's goodness towards you, how sinful you are but because of God's forgiveness you received power to do his work. Sometimes God wants to speak to us but we are cast down. Let us arise to God's expectation, arise eat and let your soul live. Sometimes, he wants to prove you, to see how much you love him. Although he already knows, he wants to put you to the test. Your task may seem difficult at times but let us submit ourselves totally to God's service. It was the coal that purged the Prophet. You need to free yourself; cry out to God 'cleanse me Lord and use me' before you can accept God call to minister to those around you. You must be clean. The method may seem painful but the process is necessary.

My Healer

This is one of the most unforgettable times in my life (approximately ten plus years ago), on Tuesday Morning of February 17, 1997, two days after arriving home from the hospital with a new born baby boy. At around 10am that morning, I felt a sharp pain pressing just above my upper left breast and the only thing I could do was breathe that holy name "Jesus". There is great power in that name. The 911 was call was made and upon the arrival of the Paramedics, they immediately took me to a near by hospital. I was at the hospital from 10:30am to 6:00pm before they could find out what my problem was; as they were doing a whole lot of different tests on me and every test they did it turn up negative. At 6:00pm, a doctor came and said to me that all the tests that had been taken so far had showed up negative; however, there was one more blood test result they are waiting on and should that one also comes out negative they will sent me home. A few minutes later he came back to me, the result is in, and unfortunately we found out that you had suffered from a mild heart attack. After been diagnosed, I was taken to the Intensive Care Unit (ICU) where I was restricted to bed rest. I was just recovering from a cesarean surgery, had three young children at home including a six days old child and my blood pressure just kept escalating. In spite of what was happening around me I had to be very calm due to the rapid escalating of my blood pressure. I was told that I was at a danger zone for a lot of things. My husband had arranged babysitting schedules, including one of my sisters and my best friend who had volunteered, in order to give my family round the clock service. I was cared for greatly, both physically and spiritually. The health care team had taken very good care of me, my church family was praying for me and God was also taking care of my healing; at this point, I had to keep focus both on my wellness and on God. God is really a mystical God and his ways are passed finding out. During my third night at the hospital, at the approach of day break, I had a vision. During the vision, I was singing this hymnology – "Amazing Grace shall always be my song of praise; for it was grace that brought my liberty. I may never know just why he came to love me so. He looks beyond my faults and saw my needs." I awoke from my sleep still praising God and singing he look beyond my faults and saw my needs, when the nurse came in to check on me as she was finishing her last round. After checking my blood pressure she looked at me, smiled and said you're doing great. Your blood pressure is back to normal. Just hearing those words from the nurse, I felt a joyful feeling deep down inside of me, I said "O Lord this is real, you've look beyond my fault and saw my needs." I felt the unction of going home. About two hours later the cardiologist came in and he said I'm happy to see your progress; you can now be downgraded to the step down unit, meaning that I could be transferred to an ordinary unit. The psalmist David declared, O Lord our God, how excellent is thy great name and power in all the earth. The doctor also broke strange news to me in that 65% of my artery was blocked and that I was one of the youngest individuals to be diagnosed with this condition. He continued saying that 'you've made history'; then smile. He said 'You will need to have a surgery done and I understand that you currently have an incision so we won't rush you right away but we urge you to have it done as soon as possible. The surgeon is not in today but he will be in tomorrow, he will come and have a talk with you.' The next day the surgeon came to see me with five of his students, he then educated me with all the necessary information and procedures, which were as follows: You have three options here, your first option is that you can be on tablets for the rest of your life; which I would not recommend because you are too young for that, plus there will be side effect. Secondly, you can have an angioplasty balloon inserted, and lastly a bypass surgery. He further said that 'your heart is not bad and your dent is as small as a rice grain; however, during the insertion, should there be any occurrences we would have to give you a bypass surgery. You are too young to be on tablets, your heart is not bad to give you a bypass surgery, so I do recommend that you take the angioplasty balloon surgery. He then asked me how I felt about this and I said, 'I am very sorry doctor, but I am not going to accept any of those offers'. He was very surprised to my respond so he tried to persuade me but after he realized how determine I was they left the room. I had a 100% confidence of my healing for God had look beyond my faults and saw my needs. There were two more doctors that came in my room still asking me to accept the surgery. I am not a very talkative person but I could feel the boldness, the power, authority to speak, more faith and confidence in God towards my healing. I was looking out the window where I saw a few trees still under the weather, because we were at the latter part of February, and I got a message from those trees. I said to the doctors "can you see those trees out there don't they look lifeless?" to which they replied yes. I continued and said 'well it's only a matter of weeks for these trees to get revived and come alive as God shall puts on their new leaves. My reason for this comment was to let the doctors know that for me having surgery was not an option. I may not be well currently but in a little while I shall be made whole. Still conversing with the doctors I said, the God that allows the trees to put on new leaves lets them bloom and come alive in its season is the one that made me and all my organs, including my arteries. Every repair that needed to be done in this body he is able to fix and that which needed to be fix in me would be fixed. He can heal that which needs to be healed. He is the same God of all creation, he made man and all that there is on this earth. One of them said to me you seem to believe in miracles? I said 'you bet I do!' He then asked the question 'would you like to see your son go through university?' I responded yes, he then said 'If you accept the surgery we would be adding to your life forty years.' I responded that that sounds really good but God already promised me eternal life because he died that I might have life and have it more abundantly. In concluding he said 'well, since you refused having the surgery, we will have to discharge you. I said that is fine with me, so they left my room feeling very disappointed in me. It wasn't an act of attitude; neither was I trying to be difficult. I knew the doctors really had my best interest at heart, especially for my kids, but I had to listen to the voice of the Lord. I left that hospital by faith claiming my healing. Day by day God gave me a new supply of strength. Two weeks after getting home from the hospital I called for a day of fasting at my home. For six consecutive months I had to do a monthly assessment. Upon each visit they would write me a prescription, which I never been filled, I would put them in my bible (which I still have up to this day). The night before my last visit with the specialist, during the six months, I had a vision. In the vision, I had a phone call from a doctor saying that he had an emergency surgery to be done on me and I should get to the office immediately. In my vision, I found myself at the doctor's office where he told me he is going to perform a surgery; it will be painless but I will experience some weakness he said. I noticed all of the instruments in the room were stainless steel. He picked an instrument in the shape of a crochet needle which was inserted in my groin. I cried out in my sleep "O my God this was the angioplasty balloon surgery that I was suppose to do". I just love the way God perform his surgery, "a surgery without a scar" When I woke up that morning I was filled with amazement I could hardly contain myself. God had given me the confirmation of my healing. That morning I could hardly wait to get to my appointment. When I had my test done, the doctor questioned me 'what have you been doing? Have you been taking those medications?' I said no, I just keep praying, he replied well just keep on doing what you're doing because you are ok. You don't have to come again to see me. You can climb Mount Everest with a smile, he said; you can visit your family doctor for any other reason but trust me you are fine. I shouted out "Hallelujah, my God you are real!" The doctor said 'what happen are you ok?' I said yes doctor I'm just worshipping God for he has been mighty good to me. When I got in to the elevator I said to my husband "please hold the baby, let me give the Lord my miracle praise because I had made a promise to the Lord that when he healed me that where ever I was I would kneel on the ground and worship him. There were people getting on and off the elevator but I didn't care I was just giving the Lord some crazy praise. When I think of God's goodness towards me, how he came in such an awesome way and healed me of my diseases; I must give him all the praise. The devil wanted me dead with even a six days old infant behind to receive no mother's care but God said you shall not die. You shall live, you shall be a testimony to many people both far and near to strengthen those that are weak and to bring them out of their difficult situations. That others may know that I am the healer of every sickness and every disease - the physical, the social, the psychological and the spiritual. Sometimes your healing might not come through right away but wait on your God; he is coming through for you. Just remember that Job had to wait timely and patiently for his healing. I could hardly wait to get into the house of God to give my testimony of praise. When I got into God's sanctuary, downloaded my testimony and my praise; God's presence overflowed and filled the atmosphere. No wonder David said 'O magnify the Lord with me and let us exalt his name together'. David also said in Ps.16:11 "...in thy presence is fullness of joy; at thy right hand there are pleasures forevermore".

I did go to my family doctor, because I had to report to him letting him know what had happened; however, when I got there he started questioning me. He told me that he had received my file and wanted to know why I didn't do the surgery. I let him know that there was no need for it; I am healed. He told me that "I will have to give you the tablets" and I said, "with due respect doctor, suit yourself, but if you write me that prescription I won't be filing it'. He wasn't pleased but when God touches you, heals you, delivers you, you don't need anyone to tell you that you are heal. When God healed the lame man, that was at the gate beautiful, Peter and John didn't have to tell him that he was healed but he got up and started leaping and praising God. So you don't need an approval when you are healed because you just don't feel the same; that touch will manifest itself. When God fills you with the Holy Ghost, you don't need any one to tell you that you are filled with the Holy Ghost. There is a complete change in your life for the indwelling power ignites your soul and keeps it alive. I trust this testimony will touch your life. Don't be afraid to seek God first; then he will direct you and give you the right leading. I allow myself to be available to God so when anyone asks me to fast and pray with them, I never say no. I am desirous of reaching out to others. God has used me in many ways and many times to fast and pray with others. God has delivered them from their sicknesses and brought them out of their situations. Sometimes the conditions seemed impossible but God always comes through for his people. Faith is the master of it all. Heb. 11:6 says without faith it is impossible to please God.

The Great Way Maker

We may often read, teach study, maybe preach or hear about how God brought the children of Israel out of bondage. We've heard how they had suffered by the hand of Pharaoh, King of Egypt, and how God made the way for them through Moses to bring them out of their suffering. You could see that there was a big difference between the Egyptian and the Hebrews who obtain the name Israelites, as the bible stated in Gen.32:24-28 when Jacob wrestled with the angel, prevailed and the angel said unto him thy name shall be no more called Jacob, but Israel. When you want God to do the job for you, you've got to be still and know that he is God; that there is no one else that can work it out. There was also a difference with their worshipping; the Israelites worshipped only one God (who is the almighty God the God of Abraham, the God Isaac, and the God of Jacob.) While the Egyptians worshipped several gods. They also had a deeply rooted culture as well as they were builders. And the Hebrews were shepherds who resided in land of Goshen.

In cultural centers, slavery was an ancient practice used by almost all nations who conquered people. Most likely the great pyramids of Egypt were built by slaves. I can imagine that there were all different levels of slavery, as every one possessed different knowledge and skills or professions such as carpenters, tent makers, masons, jewelers, or craftsmen. I do believe that regardless of their skills, or level of experience, all slaves were watched very closely by ruthless task masters, or supervisors, whose assignment was to keep the slaves working as fast and as hard as possible; this would make their lives most miserable. But in spite of every situation or circumstance, God always has a man, a divine way or some medium to come through for us. Ex.2:1-25 tells us about Moses and gives us his personal profile; that when a decree was given out by the king of Egypt that all baby boys at the age of two years old and under should be killed (as long as they were children of the Hebrews), he was put in an Ark made up of bulrushes, daubed with slime and pitch and was laid in the flags by the river brink. He was rescued by Pharaoh's daughter and was nurtured as her own son. He was educated in all knowledge and wisdom of the Egyptians and mighty in words and deeds. It came to pass when he acknowledged the children of Israel, visited them, saw their oppression and he moved with compassion towards them to defend them. I do believe for every desperate need or situation that there has to be a desperate measure taken. Act.7:37 states that "a prophet shall the Lord your God raise up unto you of your brethren, like unto me; him shall he here." Here Moses was predestinated for his calling. Rom. 8:28-29 mentions that all things works together for good to them that love God, to them who are the called to his purpose. For whom he did foreknow, he also did predestinate. As Moses was a ruler, a leader and a prophet, although Moses made excuses because he felt inadequate for the job God asked him to do. It was very natural for him to feel that way because he was inadequate all by himself. God wasn't asking him to work alone; he offered him resources to help him, which was God himself, Aaron and the ability to work miracles. God often calls us to perform tasks that seem too difficult; however, he doesn't ask us to do them alone. God offers us his resources, just as he did to Moses. You should not try to hide behind your inadequacy, as others do, but look beyond yourself to the great resources available; then you can allow God to use your unique contribution. Sometimes in the work place managers, supervisors or foremen are caught in the middle of work overload. They are pressured and been frustrated; they may try to get the people to work under pressure so that their productive may exceed more than the normal amount. There may be times that they have to do mandatory over-time and, if they do complain, disciplinary action would be taken. As such, things would likely get harder. Sometimes you too may get caught up in the middle of frustration, pressure, confusion, feel pressed out of measure, and overloaded with complaints. When this happens, you start downloading your situation on innocent folks sometimes on your spouse, your family, your neighbor, your church members, or even your leaders. But complaining or turning on leaders and innocent people doesn't solve the problem; God have a larger purpose in mind for your situation. So rather than turning on the leadership and others to have your way when you feel pressured, turn to God to see what else he might be doing about your situation. When God is at work our suffering steps back, defeat steps back and circumstances gives way. Hardship may still occur but James 1:2-4 encourages us to be happy when difficulties come your way. Problems may develop your patience and character by teaching you to trust God to do what is best for you.

I am the youngest of nine siblings and by the time I started high school my older siblings had already left home. Some had migrated to other countries while some worked and lived in the city. My mother would care for some of my nieces and nephews which had made life much better for me having children of my own age to interact with. At the age of ten I accepted the Lord Jesus Christ as my personal Savior, by baptizing in the Name of Jesus Christ for the removal of my sins and be filled with the Holy spirit according to the scriptures St. Mark 16:16 and Act. 2:38.

Becoming a Christian did not interfere with the education gold setting, but fill with excitement, having strong commitment, and changing of lifestyle which includes attending regular Sunday services, some week nights, and early Morning Prayer service as early as 5.am. Fasting and bible studies have always been my pursuit which enhances my spiritual growth wherewith I developed a passion to entreat others to Christ and intercede for the sick and afflicted. One of my lifestyle's changing were for example, all females was required to have their heads covered according to 1Cor.11:5-16. Of which my peers at school always have a problem with my head being covered; so they would sometimes pulled my hat off my head and throw it away. Some times they would return it back to me and some time not. I would always pray about it and also testified about my problem when I went to church. On this particular morning, very close to school, unexpectedly a girl came from behind me pulled off my hat and threw it over the fence; it was very upsetting. Others looked at me very strange and wondered why I didn't retaliate but I wouldn't lower my Christian character to retaliate to bring about a confrontation; but rather I resisted the temptation to take justice into my own hands. God weighed the deed and allowed one of my friend to step in for me, her words to the conflict maker was "If you think you're bad touch her again". From that day my problem had ceased; no one interfered with me wearing my hat any more. God had fought my battle and victory was mine. I just love when God comes in the midst of a situation and changed the devil's plan. David writes in Ps.27:5-6 "For in the time of trouble he shall hide me in his pavilion: in the secret of his tabernacle shall he hide me; he shall set me up upon a rock. And now shall mine head be lifted up above mine enemies round about me."

Who knows the mind of God or what plan he has set out for our lives? He is the only one that both previews and determines our lives because he is the master of tomorrow and the one who holds the future.

Immediately after finishing high school, my parents sent me to stay with one of my elder sisters that was living in the city. This wasn't an easy task for my parents to do, as being the youngest of the family, there was a very strong attachment with them. For life with my parent was just "happy go lucky".

Life in the city was quite different, let me say a very interesting time of my life, my sister had a family of seven and my extension made it eight. I made myself very flexible, and available in assisting my sister with her daily tasks; notwithstanding, church was my lifestyle. I was involved with various activities at church. I was the secretary for the Youth Department, the secretary for the Lady's Department, a member of the choir and an assistant Sunday School teacher. A demonstrator of the word of God, as being directed by him, I was very committed to the work of God. Sunday morning Educational bible studies, Evangelistic Service, Youth Service, Lady's Service, - Educational Bible Class, - Friday nights - Prayer Service (and some times all night Prayer Service), Saturday - Choir Rehearsal. I was committed to be there for all of these services. Every Wednesday I devoted as my fasting day.

One of my main parity moving into the city to live with my sister was to pursue with my careers. But unfortunately there were not much job opportunities for job seekers. During that time, I was experiencing some wear and tear with my clothes and shoes including one pair of slippers that I had brought up with me from the country.

The tip of the heels was gone, and if I should walk too hard it would've made a very funny sound - "cong, cong, cong". I would try to be very cautious with the pressure of my steps so that not much sound would be heard from my shoes as I walked on the street. As for my slippers, I had taken them to the shoemaker and had him dyed it from brown to black so that others might think I had a new pair of slippers. I didn't want to ask my sister to assist me with my needs because it was just her husband who was working at the time; so, I really didn't want to pressure them in any way. Neither did I want my parents to know what was going on because I know that they would tell me that I should come home to them. When children are born they are completely dependent upon their parents for all their basic necessities, this may cause some parents to forget that these same children will grow towards independence within the span of a few short years. Being sensitive to the different stages of that healthy growth will greatly strengthen family relationships and resisting or denying that process will cause great pain. We should gradually let go of our children, in order to allow them to face the real world and to become mature as independent adults.

My sisters said to me one day that I should go into her closet and take for myself one of her best shoes. I was indeed thrilled for the offer but there was a great problem with the sizing; my feet are one size above hers. Anyhow, I settled for one of them. These shoes were very gorgeous but very tightly fitted; as I said we had a size problem. The primary problem I had with these shoes was that as long as

I was up and going it would be ok but the moment I sat in a relaxing position it would be very uncomfortable. It was always a treat for me when a chorus would be raised in church and worshipping was at the highest peak or, in other word, if I had to be in a standing position then my discomfort would ease. I avoided taking them off because getting them on again would be quite a task. I have never been a complainer, but a prayer warrior as Paul said in whatever state he finds himself he'll be content. He also said he knew how to abound and how to abase. So amides the circumstances way down in my heart I felt blessed because I was a child of the king. But what he was doing here? He was breaking me, molding me, making me and preparing me for tomorrow and for the real world.

I and two other friends would always go job seeking together but at the end of the day we would accomplish nothing." At this point, I was at the breaking point of my situation. I said to myself that enough is enough and I started talking to God about my situation. I looked back at the children of Israel and how God had made great ways for them. I thought of his kindness and the favor he shows towards them. I also thought of how ungrateful the children of Israel were to God, how they provoked God to anger and how God destroyed them. I said 'God, please allow me to keep my promise to you. I would like you to make a way for me as you did for the children of Israel and although they have forgotten you, I will never forget you.' So every now and then I make sure I examine myself to see how much I am keeping up to that promise with God. I can assure you when God makes a promise he always keep them and so should we. I guess God had some greater plans for me and that it would only a matter of time for me to find it out. I just can't forget that Saturday night as I knelt by my bedside and started praying. I was talking to God as if he was kneeling beside my bedside. These were my exact words as I questioned God, "God, are you still around your throne? Do you still remember your own? Are you still working miracles? Well, God, if you're still around your throne and you still remember your own and you're still working miracles then I would like you to work one for me. Lord I have relatives in the United State of America; they are just aunts, uncles and cousins so I don't want to go there. I do not want to go back to the country; I would like to go to Canada where my sisters are. My two sisters had promise to sponsor me. I wrote to them two letters and neither of them responded to my letters. God thou knowest all things about me, you know that I can be very embarrassed when I ask of favors and it wasn't granted. Dear God, the only way I get to Canada is if you make the way for me. So, can you trouble them for me at this time? As I repeatedly kept saying these words "trouble them at this time", I saw a hand of a lady, very oriental from the elbow to the fingers, stretched out -wards with a red telephone receiver. I didn't hear the conversation but I started praising God. O give thanks unto the Lord for he is good. In Ps.40:1-4, David received four benefits for waiting on God. He was lifted up out of despair, had his feet set on a rock giving him a firm place to stand, and had a new song put in his mouth. Often times, blessings cannot be received unless you go through the trial of waiting. I can truly say blessed be God who had inclined his ears unto my cry.

After I finished praying and went into my bed I felt very nervous. I heard a voice say to me 'Don't doubt God. You asked him to work a miracle for you and He has done it'. At 6:00am the next morning, surprisingly, was my eldest brother came to the house, my brother in-law said to him what are you doing here so early? He responded saying 'I woke up from twelve o clock last night from a dream where I saw my little sister praying and crying that she doesn't want to go back to the country but she want the Lord to make a way for her. I am here to let her know that

God is going to bless her and when God starts blessing her he won't stop. God is real. He is a miracle working God. He is good and he is indeed wonderful. There is no God like unto my God. He is just altogether lovely. I ran out of my room, and I hugged my brother and it was just tears of joy coming down my cheeks. Oh thank you Jesus, you are truly amazing and you're kind. With mixed feelings, I blessed the Almighty God. One shouldn't underestimate God's messengers; whom God chooses to tell his secrets. God spoke through the dumb ass for Balaam to realize that God was speaking. God spoke to my brother who was not saved in order for me to believe that He had done the job. I didn't open up to my brother to share with him my experience because he wasn't saved then but right there God was working a way out for him to be saved because he left him with a great testimony of which I didn't understand then. Approximately three days after he came by to deliver a message that was coming from one of my sisters saying that she wanted to see me very urgently. When I got by her house she told me this amazing thing that there was a job for her in Canada but she wouldn't be able to go because her daughter was too young to be left alone. She turned to me and said, "Do you think you could go in my place". My answer was "yes". Within me was just joy bubbling over; I was experiencing the other side of God. God does work in mysterious ways, His wonders to perform. I was asked to attend an interview and when I got to the interview what I saw on the kitchen counter was a red telephone. I opened my eyes in amazement and I said to myself 'my God how much crazier can this get?' I felt like screaming out loud "Glory to God, hallelujah". The family was oriental just like what I saw while I was praying. The interviewer told me that her husband's sister just had a baby with an expectation of returning to work in six months time and would like me to be there for that time. The family was business oriented so they are well known in the country. It is said that it's not who you know but it's who knows you. Because they were well known, my documents were taken care of very promptly and they informed the authorities to put all my documents on rush. They arranged for all my appointments and interviews. In the space of six months all my particulars were taken care of including all expenses. God had placed me with a nice caring family, I couldn't desire more. Two weeks after I was settled down, I decided to give one of my sisters a call and when she answered the phone she greeted me nicely and she also enquired of the rest of the family at home. I replied by saying that I'm fine and when I was leaving around two weeks ago they were fine. She asked me where I was and I told her I was in Canada. She cried out oh my God, oh my God, and couldn't believe it. How did you get here she asked? I told her it was God who made the way for me to be here, she was really in great shock. It doesn't matter what you're going through; don't quit and don't give up. It doesn't matter how rough it may seems to be, God can come through for you. I claim him to be my miracle working God and I trust you do the same too. He is my great deliverer and, more so, he is my great way maker. There is none like him. Continue to fight through your situation because it's not really over unless God says so.

He Is Always There

There will be times when you might feel discouraged and all alone with heavy burdens weighing you down; broken hearted and even cast down. At times you don't even care to share your situation with anyone because way down in your heart you're saying who would even care to listen to me or who will I be able to put my trust and confidence in? Is there anyone able to keep my situation confidential? Folks these days do not maintain confidentiality. Some will go as far as to tell you it will be just between you and them or they might say to you that it will never leave their mouth; however, it might stay confidential for that moment you are around them but it is only a matter of time before they reach for that cell phone or send that text or e-mail. So instead of your situation staying confidential, it becomes a rumor. So because of one person's mistrust, you may drag yourself to a certain dimension feeling like someone that is suffocating because of a state of impact or like one that is experiencing respiratory depression; it doesn't matter what you may do or don't do, it won't get you anywhere. You may feel worthless, doubtful or even dreadful. You don't even feel as obligated as usually in sharing your problems with anyone but if you should who would listen anyway? It is so desperate and fearful to feel like you are in a world by yourself. But it doesn't have to be this way there is a solution. The reason for you to tell your problems to someone is for you to release your troubled mind and for someone to pray you through; so that you can be strengthen and be yourself again. In order to have a healthy environment everyday we collect our garbage and put it aside for the garbage collector so that they can take care of it. Now your surrounding is clean and fresh. So it is when you get rid of your depression, anger, frustration, confusion and your messed up mind. In order for your mind to be clean and pure, someone else can find pleasure in recycling it. It's ok. Don't feel, as if you had done something bad. God have delivered you from that situation and he said to cast all your care upon him for he careth for you. Sometimes, you may be referred to councilors and sometimes councilors themselves need to be counseled by someone. They too are experiencing stress and are not problem-free. So, when you seek counseling be sure you get the right one. Let us also look for ways to honor God in our current circumstances for God will not abandon us. Let us also look towards God's plans for us. He promised us that he will never leave us nor forsake us. In every situation there's an answer for every problem. Sometimes we are faced with small problems and sometimes great problems. Small problems always need small answers but when we are face with great problems, God can exercise his great power. How big are your problems? No matter how great your problems seem to be you trust God. God can handle it. Big problems just put you in the perfect position to watch God give you a big answer. He is the prayer answering God.

You Shall Be Rewarded According As Your Work

Every good investor would seek to find the best financial institute and a financial adviser by whom he or she can be fully advised as to what package to take or the best way to invest their money. They would also try to seek out the terms and conditions on their interest rate and whether or not they are going to have a locked rate or one of the variable rates. Whatever choice you make, your interest is to know that your investment is growing and at the end of the day you will be rewarded. This is the way every positive Christian ought to be. To be concerned about their Christian welfare; in seeking some of the best ways to grow spiritually of which a Christian's base foundation of investment should be fasting, prayer and daily reading of the word of God. By doing so, you will gain much strength, motivation and have much room for growth because you're working towards your reward which is eternal life. You may not find yourself at the same level everyday. Some times you will be very strong and motivated in the Lord so that you can speak to every mountain that stands before you and have the faith that at the mention of the name of Jesus it shall be removed. There will be times when you may seem cast down and some what disquieted. You may wonder if you were the same person yesterday and may feel like one that has backslidden from God's standard of righteousness; As David made mention in Ps. 42:5-8 Why art thou cast down, O my soul? And why art thou disquieted in me? Hope thou in God: for I shall yet praise him for the help of his countenance. O my God my soul is cast down within me: there will I remember thee from the hill Mizar. Deep calleth unto deep at the noise of thy waterspouts: all thy billows are gone over me. Yet the Lord will command his loving-kindness in the daytime, and in the night his song shall be with me, and my prayer unto the God of my life. As, you continue seeking the Lord for him to strengthen you and revive your soul again. The scripture also said that we should sing hymns and spiritual songs, making melodies in our hearts unto the Lord. Because when your mind is not on the Lord it is some where else and you are liable to slip. So, it is with your investment. There will be times when the interest rate will be very high and it seems as if things are going very well for you and you may think to yourself that you wish you had put more in your investment. Also, there will be times when the interest rate will drop very low and mess things up leaving you wondering what's next. There may even be times when the company might go bankrupt; then comes disappointment for all your life's savings because it is down the drain and you had accomplished nothing. The "reward of your savings is lost". Life can be very challenging. At times there will be some dull moments but you just can't give up, you will just have to go on. So, should you at any time feel drained, hopeless, empty and flat, just remember Ps.18:32-34. God promised to give you strength to meet up with every challenge but he doesn't promise to eliminate them. If he gives you no rough road to walk, no mountain to climb and no battles to fight, you would not grow. He will not leave you alone with your challenges but he will stand by you, teach you and help you to face them. Sometimes, situations will face you, while you are going through your challenges but when those moments come just focus your thoughts on your reward which awaits you in glory. If you should neglect the services of the Lord, accept being influence by your friends, accept the bad thoughts, listen to the voices that come to your mind, or accept the attraction of the worldly goods more than the righteousness of God, then you would surely delay your righteous progress with God. But, if you should be willing to listen and obey the voice of God, comply with his will and be dedicated to him in order to fulfill that great requirement, then surely all the promises he made unto you will come your way. O how joyful it is to be dwelling in God's will and to enjoy the rich blessings which he has in store for those who achieve their accomplishments. All great accomplishments come through great service, willingness, self-sacrifice, obedience, love and a good mind to follow God. You may encounter with some weary days and restless nights, some discouragements, hardship and even false brethren, but whatever you may face, or you are currently going through, above all, be the best of whatever you are. We will all have to stand before the judgment seat of God (Ro.14:10) and shall be accountable for our self. Also, we shall be rewarded according as our works or the life we display before God. Each person will be accountable to Christ not to others; so, we have to be straightforward on our Christian walk for life. Looks can be very deceptive, although you may be complimented on your physical looks but the real beauty is behind that look.

The real you is within. Beauty, however, begins inside a person. A gentle, modest, loving character gives a light to the face that cannot be duplicated by the best of cosmetics and jewelry in the world because a carefully groomed and well decorated exterior is artificial and cold unless inner beauty is present. So looks do not really determine who we really are. Sometime someone may try to categorize you and say 'oh, you look like a Minister, a Pastor, a Missionary, an Evangelist, a Christian, a church brother, or a church sister'. In whatever category you may fall, just examine yourself as you question 'am I really what I'm suppose to be?' Not what I really look like Lord, but what I'm really suppose to be. To have a resemblance doesn't identify the object or the person you should be. Try to stay real for God already knows who you are and false identities will be unacceptable in the achievement of reward on the final Day of Judgment. Therefore, your reward is sure. There will be no bogus documentation, or duplicate; it shall be real because God is real. Sometimes your place of employment may mess up the payroll system, so you could not get the pay for your wages but God will not mess up his payroll, because His records are always up to date; he will not forget your pay. Seeing then that we shall be judged by our work, let us be steadfast and be sober, as Eph.5:15-16 tell us that we should walk circumspectly, not as fool but as wise; redeeming the time because the days are evil.

Giving injustice to a situation to satisfy someone else's negligence is wrong, for being justified by faith we shall have peace with God. Be realistic! Justice should be given to who it is due. You should be sensitive to the needs of others; give some encouragement and offers supportive words (especially to those who labor among you). It doesn't matter what their ministry titles are. Ph.4:3 said to remember those women which labored in the Gospel. These women must have been some very hard workers for

Christ in the church. So you should remember especially those that are over you in the Lord; they should receive due respect, double honor or be highly esteem. You're probably thinking it is a great task and wondering how it can be accomplished but it not a great task and it is very simple. Just express your appreciation to your pastor and leaders; let them know you have been helped by their leadership, their teaching, the demonstrations of the word of God through their preaching, and for ministering in to your life. Let them feel good knowing that they are doing a good work, as it is said that good encouragement strengthens labor. Have you ever been to church and feeling very sick, or discourage, and by listening to the demonstration of the word of God through the preacher your sickness or other situation is change even before the ending of the service? If you sit and say nothing, how then will they know where you stand? Just remember they are always at the forefront; they need and deserve your love. They also need your support not because they are leaders but because they too need admonishing, encouragement, to be embraced; someone to let them know how well they brought forth the word, ask them to keep up the good work and also pray for them so that God will endow them with a fresh anointing. If you haven't been doing this, you should start doing so because at the end of the day you need them and they need you. By doing so, your leader will glorify God for allowing them to be of great blessing to others and, at the same time, you will be rewarded for your good deeds. You should know what spiritual benefits you are receiving from your leaders and that you cannot pay them for their works, the pay off is at the end of their life's journey which God, who is their master, will reward them. Remember that they are toiling for you though thick and thin, good times and bad time, in ailments and good health, through spiritual warfare, strongholds and turmoil, through storms, sunshine and rain, having no mind of giving up. Amidst the hard tasks they just keep toiling for those whom the Holy Ghost had made them overseer. When you are sleeping, they are toiling, praying and studying the word of God to distribute to the hungry soul. There will be times when you are dining at the breakfast table that they are fasting and praying so that God will give them a new revelation and extra strength in their ministry. It is said that good encouragement strengthen labor, does this sound anything like you?

Sometimes we are so tight handed or feel pressured when it comes to offering time, never mind when a special offering has been requested but it is said that it is so much better to give than to receive. I can share this testimony with you, One Sunday Morning, on my to church, I said to my husband I have no money but this fifty dollars to take me to work for the week, however, a voice keeps telling me to give it for my offering. My husband didn't respond, so upon that note I gave it for my offering. Surprisingly, while socializing after service, a Sister placed in my hand a fifty dollars bill. I was stunned for a moment. It was just unbelievable that I had received 100% of what I had given. The scripture said that God loveth a cheerful giver and also said give and it shall be given back to you and I have experienced that for myself. So, the next time when you are giving your offering give it freely for you never know what the Lord might do for you. Not only with money but always give unto the Lord willing services and with the willingness of your heart; He will bestow upon you his richest blessing. Be observant when it comes to leaders, for in them lies great benefits. Every eye is always on them and they have to account for every believer that is under their leadership. They have to be accountable of every office, and activity that is performed; even when they ask someone else to be in charge of it. They are great mentors, teachers, preachers, caretakers, councilors and much more because as God promotes, or elevates, them he also gives them new levels of operation. Do you hold the office of a Spiritual Leader, or you would like to become one some day? Well, see 1 Ti.3:1-12. The standard is very high and you must meet the high expectations and its great ability. However, their hard work and accomplishments shall win them a great crown of righteousness, if they faint not. Just think of these words "If you faint not". Can you imagine after doing all this great task and at the end when you come for your reward and you do not hear "well done" but your reward is "depart from me I know you not"? What a great disappointment that would be! Remember in Deut. 34 how God took Moses up from the plains of Moab unto the mountain of Nebo and showed him all the other cities; after such hard labor, he didn't receive a reward of well done. Knowing how great a leader Moses was, the only one who spoke to God face to face (Ex. 33:11); yet, this great man was not allowed to enter the Promised Land because he disobeyed God (Num.20:12). It doesn't matter how good we are or how much we have done for God, we sometimes disobeyed him. The result of our disobedience is that we will be disciplined. So it definitely behooves us to be careful for nothing as 1Cor.15:58 say that we should be steadfast, unmovable, always abounding in the work of the Lord, forasmuch as ye know that your labor is not in vain in the Lord.

Victory Is Ahead

There will be some point or time in your life that you might experience some type of defeat which might cause you some embarrassment, or low self-esteem. No one would like to be a victim, to be embarrassed, to be defeated, or conquered by the enemy; rather, we want to be the victor over every foe. This is a good motive only to be enforced. As you trod along life's way, defeat is the last word you want to have in mind; even when thing not going right. You should release your thoughts by saying victory is ahead. Sometimes you might experience great sickness, or affliction, for many years where you cannot get well and no doctor can comprehend your sickness. Discouragement, frustration and other thoughts may crowd your mind, but amidst everything you keep holding on to faith for your victory and your deliverance. Sometimes, prolonged illness may weaken your faith by causing you to think that God is not hearing you or prayer doesn't seem to be working out for you and that nothing seems to be working. As human tendency, we do get impatient and may even ask "O Lord Jesus how long?" Although, sometimes you may consider that some sickness, make life seems unfair but if you only trust God and believe that with him all things are possible; loneliness, disappointment and death may cause you to say that God will surely show up for you. Suffering may be visible but he made a promise that he will not allow you to go through more than what you can bear. For when God shows up for you he will do two things, either heal you completely from your illness (so that you can have a testimony to share with others that they too will know that Jesus Christ is the great healer) or what God might do is take you out of the sickness. Not that your condition was too critical for him to deal with, for with God all things are possible nor is there any thing too hard for God to do (Gen.18:14, Jer.32:18), but he does what's best for you. In such cases, you will be free from all heartaches, pain, sicknesses, sorrows and complaints. But in either way, God had come through for you, by healing you from the situation or by taking you out of the situation. So in any case, you're victorious for God defeated the purpose of sickness and has given victory over every sickness. Job 14:14 reminded us of when Job was going through his suffering that, although his sickness made him uncomfortable, he knew he would not have been in his conditions forever. He knew it was only a matter of time before God would come through for him; he could see his change coming. He said all the days of his appointed time he will wait until his change come. It doesn't matter what you may face in life; it is good to hold on to courage, knowing that help is coming for you. You may not see it physically but with patience, hope and trust wait for your release. You can even see here that Job wasn't even putting the blame on God for what he was going through; as he was very expressive in chapter 13:14-15. "Wherefore do I take my flesh in my teeth, and put my life in my hand? Though he slay me, yet will I trust in him: but I will maintain mine own ways before him." Just in case you didn't know, the very best comforter you can ever find in this world is yourself. It doesn't matter what great words folks may say to you, while you are going through your circumstances, it may not register to your mind at once. However, when you start comforting yourself and accepting what God allows, a whole lot of things start to disappear and great changes appears; different attitudes and mindsets begin to appear regarding your condition. You gain peace of mind and stop blaming folks or God for what happening to you. You will also find room for acceptance and giving of thanks. Right there you will start gaining your victory. Ps. 23:4 says "Yea, though I walk through the valley of the shadow of death, I will fear no evil, for thou art with me, thy rod and thy staff they comfort me." There are two great key words in this verse of psalm "rod and staff". We understand that a rod is always use for correction, while the staff is a sustainer, or the bread of life; so then, if it pleases God to correct you with sickness or affliction, how much worse can it get "down in the valley of the shadow of death"? Nevertheless, be not afraid because he is beside you with his staff leading you, sustaining you and strengthening you with great comforting words. Although he slay me yet will I trust him. If by any chance you are encountering a sin sick disease that has you confused to where you just can't forgive yourself for what you have done and you would like to get rid of it but don't know how? Surrender it to God! Now is the time. Whether you are a hit man, an abuser, a murderer, a drug addict, a thief, a robber or it is so horrible that society refuses to associate with you and your own family disowns you, all because of your behavior; just surrender your life to God. Is.1:18 said 'though your sins be as scarlet, they shall be as white as snow; though they be red like crimson, they shall be as wool.' So when you come to a decision with God to repent of your sins, meaning you are sorry for all of your wrong doing, accept being baptized in Jesus' name for the removal of your sin and you receive the gift of the Holy Ghost, see Act. 2:38, when you accept Jesus as your personal Savior, there will be a great difference to your life. When God reveals himself unto you, removes the scale of sin from your eyes, washes and cleanses you from your polluted state, turns your life around, he defeats the purpose of sin for a gain of God's righteous through salvation which becomes your victory over sin. Now you become a new man, old things are passed away because you are born again. 2 Co. 5:17 says therefore if any man be in Christ he is a new creature. You're of a Christian nature; you're prone to righteousness and holiness. Now the word of God becomes your sword and, instead of being a hit man, you become defense against sin. Instead of breaking the bank, you start breaking down every barrier of sin. Instead of stealing corruptible things, you steal away to God; seeking souls to be born for his kingdom. Now when folks look at you they become amazed wondering to themselves if this was the same person that used to do this and do that; but God will give you a new look. Yes, he made all things become new. He will place a different image in you, both the likeness and mind of God. Paul said let this mind be in you that was also in Christ Jesus. God changed you from the likeness of the devil and erased the devil's thoughts then replaced them with joy and gladness. He defeated the purpose of the devil and replaced it with victory. If at all this sound in any way like what God has done for you, then give God some praise and glorify him for the thing he has done for you; for the great change he has brought in your life. Feel yourself very blessed because there are so many that have die in their sins and did not get the chance to turn around. There are those whose lives have been ruined, defeated and are left to face a hellish penalty with zero chance of gaining the victory because there is no repentance in the grave. The devil will stand in your way at times ready to defeat you, to watch you fall, to cast you down, to embarrass you because he knows that there is victory in sight. So, he will try to pressure your mind, confuse your spirit and let everything go against you but if you are in a position that you can't get the chance to pray only say "Jesus, Jesus, Jesus, allow me to stand up for your victory." You may feel weak but in your weakness stand strong for God and hold on to faith with great determination for the moment you let go you will be in danger of a defeat.

Be Defensive Towards Your Victory

I can imagine how happy Satan was when he deceived Adam and Eve by having them comply with the test and fail. He thinks he had prevailed over God, but God allowed it. It was a test for mankind; to see how much trust, confidence and resistance we had against the forces of evil. Because man had failed by listening to the voice of the devil, God became very defensive against sin. In Gen. 3:14-19, God had cursed the serpent above all cattle and above every beast of the field; upon thy belly shall thou go and dust shall thou eat all the days of thy life. Unto Eve he said 'she shall greatly multiply her sorrow and conception, and in sorrow she shall bring forth children'. Unto Adam he said 'cursed is the ground for thy sake; in sorrow shall thou eat of it all the days of thy life'. We as Christians have to be very defensive against sin, by not conceiving in any way. James 1:14-15 tells us "but every man is tempted, when he is drawn to his own lust, and enticed. Then when lust hath conceived, it bringeth forth sin: and sin, when it is finished, it bringeth forth death". You will have to put a barricade to keep out sin as authorities would have put up barricades to keep out crimes. Our sin does not always appear ugly to us and the 'pleasant' sins are the hardest to avoid. So prepare yourself for the attractive temptations. Remember that there is always a way of escape (1 Cor.10:13). Use God's word and God's people to help you stand against it. Because the battle is often lost at the first look at temptation. Temptation always begins by simply seeing something you want. Are you struggling with temptation because you have not learned that looking is the first step towards sin? You could win over temptation more often if you followed Paul's advice in 2 Tim. 2:22 that you should run from those things that produce evil thoughts. The hymnology strengthens us as it said "yield not temptations for yielding is sin, each victory will help you some other to win" So when we become defensive against all wrong doing, all bad thoughts, all ugly, evil and wicked ways we are then using our resources; most of all, the words of God which is your shield and butler and also your hiding place. You must also understand in order to survive you must conquer. God doesn't tolerate evil; neither should it be tolerated in your life. You must ruthlessly remove sin from your life before it takes control of you. Jesus Christ is your commander; so, should you be surrounded or at any time you feel that you are under attack, be ready to conquer. God has the power to conquer and to destroy as well as put all things under His feet. As you have heard the story of how God allowed Joshua and the children of Israel to bring down the walls of Jericho and its fenced city (Jos. 6:14-20), the great invincible God is superior to all gods. There is none like Him! Studies show that the city of Jericho was built thousands of years before Joshua was even born and that it was one of the oldest cities in the world. No doubt it was idolized and adored by many people but here God delivered it into the hands of Joshua to do as he commanded him to do and the people obeyed Joshua. They walked with one accord as they marched around the city for one week but on the last day some thing amazing happened; they marched around the city seven consecutive times. It was then when their victory came and the walls came down so that they could go and possessed the city. So is it in your life, unless you allow God to break down the walls of sin, then you cannot have the victory over the enemy. God's specific instructions must be carried out. What if God had asked you to go on seven days of fasting and on the seventh day you should pray seven times without stopping? My God, you would've come up with so many excuses and so many why questions - "Oh Lord, that is not necessary. "Why not one day of fasting where I pray seven times or fast seven days and pray one time?" But it's not your will but as God's will that must be done for you to get the victory; you will have to obey the command of God. Our enemy, which is Satan, has been defeated by Christ (Ro.8:37). Although we fight battles every day and sin runs rampant in the world, we have the assurance that the war has already been won. We do not have to be paralyzed by the power of a defeated enemy because we can overcome him through the power of Jesus Christ. Although the instruction that God has given you may sound strange and you may wonder what can come out of it, be obedient; even when you can't understand the logic behind God's plan. You must obey his instructions and commands in order for you to gain the victory. Sometimes, we are waiting for the battle to be won before we give God the praise. Maybe you are not too sure if God is going to come through for you but if you could only understand that God had already come through for you; then, you would be praising him. If you are not sure, all you have to do is to claim your victory by faith because it is guaranteed. If you claim it, it is yours! So, start sending up your victory praises now.

In Order To Obtain The Prize You Must Endure

Every successful athlete that obtains the winning crown had to experience some great struggles to get to the top. Not by any means that anyone would rather torture or be stressed out to become famous when the procedures are not all glamorous. Considering all the necessary criteria and the long process (never mind the commanding coach that will always push you to the limit), you may not feel strong enough to push your way towards victory but thinking of the rewards to be received at the end of the race makes you want to proceed with pleasure. Because it doesn't matter how difficult the situation gets, if there is no pleasure in doing it, it doesn't make sense you proceed. It must had been difficult at times, to rise early and settle down late at nights, to be away from families and friends (especially on some great occasions) and to say no to some great party's invitations. Even though the rules were tabled very dramatically at first; however, because of the zeal or the anxiety and the desired mine of being successful athletes with the winning crown, there was no occasion of considering any press. However, as challenges arise during the career, you realized that everyday it's a new challenge facing you. You thought more or less that the task would be challenging but not too difficult to handle, just by thinking of the commanding coach, the falls, the bruises, the injures and the frustrations the only thought that might be going through the mind is quitting. You may watch many comes and go, many falls by the way even as close as to the finish line; however, they had received nothing. They had put out much but didn't endure to the end. So it gives you great courage to go forward for the end is in sight. Sometimes as you are approaching the end of a long race, your joints may begin to hurt, your throat burns, and your legs aches; as a matter of fact, your whole body may cry out for you to stop. This is when you appreciate your family, friends and fans the most for their thoughtfulness and encouragements helps you to proceed through the pain to the finish line. That's the way we should be there to encourage one another along the Christian journey. There are some very difficult moments when a word of encouragement would be a great source of strength and support could be the difference between finishing well and collapsing along the way. But with your steadfastness in mind, you held on to with determination and confidence. Kept a positive attitude as you progressed toward success; knowing that at the end when you've run, won the race and obtain the first prize award as the world's greatest champion, how happy you will be because you had endured the struggles, the aches, the pains, the frustrations to obtain the prize. Just think of the others that have started out in the race with you and some had dropped out by the way. Some had suffered severe injuries and were unable to continue to the finish line but here you are as the winning star.

As a child coming up I thought that being a Christian was an easy walk in the park, or a bed of roses. As caring for the roses, someone will have to take the task and care for them on a daily basis - watering, pruning and grooming them. In other words, being a Christian I thought was just a smooth sliding. No sickness, no pain, sorrow, complaint, or hardship; every step of the way was just glamorous, didn't require any endurance in the way, no thorns, no thistles, no rocks to hurt the feet. Oh what great fantasy! As the poplar phrase is. "Life is just for living" and with such task of course not, we are not getting anywhere. Yes there will be rocks to hurt the feet and there will be thorns and thistles in the way. If life had no struggles, what could we possibly gain? There would be no personal testimony. There would be no joy to share and no crown filled with stars to be obtained. If you don't endure the cross, you will not gain the crown of righteousness.

The more Jesus preached and taught in the synagogues, healed the sick or worked miracles and even testified that he and his father are one they still sought to kill him (see Jn. 7:28-30 & 11:30-31). So Jesus who is the great mentor of us all endured the cross and despised the shame in order for us to obtain salvation.

The more you experience a closer relationship with Jesus, the rougher the path will be and the harder the task may seem. During your sacred times with the Lord, the devil is always busy planning ways and devices to attack and destroy your Joy. It is a fact that after a series of consecration, with fasting and prayer, you may say "Well I am filled up with new strength, Satan will have to back off"; but little did you know that Satan was in a conference figuring out how to mess up your mind and confuse your thoughts so that you will fall victim to his plans. He will try to attack your family or your job while you are busy with the Lord.

When you intercede you have to ask God to defeat his purpose and to bring down all his strongholds. Have you ever noticed when we come together in the unity of the spirit and pull down Satan and his host how messed up he is? Remember that you have got the God given right and power to put Satan and his host under feet. We can't get too comfortable when there is war around us or because we fight one battle and win makes us want to put up the sword and rest a while; no, it's a continuous battle. The more advanced you get in God; the greater the test, the bigger the promotion, the greater the pay, the hotter the battle and the sweeter the victory. Trust me, when there is no storm in your life, no test, no trials, no endurances, life is just on a smooth sail then something is going wrong. Check yourself! Don't let the devil secure you for himself. When he doesn't have you to himself, he will bring all sorts of disasters to get you down but if you resist him then he will flee. The road should not always be smooth. There will be tough times which will makes you basically feel as if it will sweep you off your feet but God will not allow that to happen to you because his eyes are upon the righteous and his ears are open up to their cry. However, he is challenging you to place you to higher ground. If we endure the chastening then God is dealing with us as sons. For what son is there whom a father loved and doesn't chasten? The key word of our testing is to "endure"; no matter what you are experiencing. Because our Christian life involves hard work, it requires us to give up whatever endangers our relationship with Christ and to be patient in our running. Do not envy others who are ahead of you because you do not know their strength, neither do you know their endurance but you know your strength. You know your endurance, your aim and desire. Many will drop out by the way and some will lie in the way but those who are determined will pursue to the end. Keep your eyes on Jesus; you will stumble if you look away from him to stare at others or at your circumstances surrounding you. You are running for Christ and you have to keep him in sight. It is very easy to lose sight of the big picture but keep focused because you are not alone; Jesus is always there. The training ground for Christians is suffering and, if you endure, it will take you to maturity which through patient will allow you to make it to your final victory.

You Will Have To Give Up To Achieve

In order to achieve the result you will have to give up worldly ties and endure rigorous discipline, like athletes we must train hard, and follow the rules. We must work extremely hard and be patient no matter what. We have to keep going despite the suffering because of the thought of victory, the vision of winning and the hope of reaping. We will see that our suffering was worth while when you achieve your goal of glorifying God. Winning people to Christ and one day living eternally with him. Paul was a persecutor of the church, in the bible days, of which some of the believers were punished to the extreme. Some were stone to death, bound and cast in prison, while some were whipped with many strips. However, Jesus revealed himself to Paul on the Damascus road of which his life was changed and so was his attitude to Christians (Acts. 9:3-20). As he stepped in the race, he realized how demanding and straight forward it was. I can't imagine just how he felt being a recipient; facing what he had allowed other to go through. He was aware of the fact that this Christian race involved some punishment, some hard trials, testing, some imprisonment and even death. It must have made his testimonies grow stronger and strengthen his desire towards endurance. Paul had a determination to do the work of the lord. It didn't matter what happened, his life was surrendered to Christ because God was depending on him to preach the gospel. So is God depending on you to live a life that is well pleasing in his sight. God is examining the work you perform before him. You should build your life on the words and let his words abide in you. The word tells us how to live for him and how to serve him. If you ignore the word of God, you will certainly be ashamed for your gain will be punishment. Be consistent and be diligent. Study God's word because it is vitally important; otherwise, you will be lulled into neglecting God and your real purpose for him. If you really want to obtain that prize, you will have to keep holding on. Probably, when Paul started, he had suffered as evil doers for the gospel sake. He was chained but the word of God is not chained. Referring to his imprisonment and being chained in shackles, but the word of God is free. He worshipped God in the prison and our powerful God loosed him from his chains. God took him out of prison because God saw his endurance. God knows what you're experiencing in your struggles. He knows what you can endure and he is able to take you to the finish line. There is great reward at the end. Paul endured as 2 Tim 2 tells us. At the end of his race, he left a testimony that he fought a good fight, he had kept the faith, he had finished his course and there laid up for him was a crown of righteousness. Not for him only but for all those who had also struggled through tests, through the fights, false imprisonment, being ridiculed by the enemy. Remember you shall also be given a crown of righteousness, if you endure to the end. Sometimes, through our struggles, we may weep because of grief and pain; sorrows or complain no money to pay your bill, you can't see our way through or no joy inside. Maybe great sickness that causes you to be terrified and doctors have given you over. There seems to be no hope. Just keep on holding on! Through the excruciating pain, through the storm, through the long night watches; remember that weeping may endure for a night but great joy awaits you in the morning (Ps. 30:5).